CW00407707

The Smooth Guide to
Fly Fishing in South and South East Spain
and the
Costa Resorts

Philip Pembroke

Phil's Fishing Guide Books

The Smooth Guide to Fly Fishing in South and South East Spain and the Costa resorts

Published by Philip Pembroke

E-mail address: philippembroke007@hotmail.com

ISBN – 13: 9780954692438

A hard copy is available to view, upon request from the British Library

The front cover shows Spanish angling enthusiast Rafa Muñoz, fly fishing for brown trout on the River Genil near Granada.

The back cover shows the River Tajo, a fantastic trout fishery near Cuenca.

Individual regions, located on the map of South and South East Spain and the Costa Resorts and highlighted, are covered by the guide book under separate chapter headings (Andalusia, Valencia and Murcia).

Contents

Where to fish ▼

For centuries Lagunas de Ruidera, in Castilla la Mancha has attracted anglers. Don Quixote didn't need a licence, but you do – details, on where to purchase one are provided under separate chapter headings.

Experience Fly Fishing in Southern Spain

Rafa Muñoz casts a fly lure on the River Castril in Granada.

Most visitors' first taste of Spain is entering through one of the busy airports serving the Costa resorts in the south and eastern parts of Spain, where one's first glimpse of water is most likely to be of a partially dry river bed colored with algal blooms.

However once you begin to explore further afield, you will be surprised and delighted to find there are many wonderful watercourses and lakes throughout south and south east Spain and the Costa resort areas, which as you will now be aware hold some outstanding trout and barbel fishing.

Spanish fly fishermen catch brown and rainbow trout, four species of barbel, American largemouth Black bass, shad, mullet, pike and carp too! And so can you, for the price of a Spanish freshwater fishing licence, which starts at just €8.

THE SMOOTH GUIDE TO FLY FISHING IN SOUTHERN SPAIN AND THE COSTA RESORTS

In many cases, just a stones throw from the Costa resorts of Málaga, Murcia and Alicante you will find, in tumbling streams, a good head of brown trout and where the underlying rock is limestone these fish grow quickly and to a considerable size, providing great sport on light fly fishing tackle.

Here too, there are some surprises including the presence of hard fighting barbel that will readily rise to brown imitation fly lures in fast flowing rivers found near València. Destructive American largemouth Black bass will go nuts for large baitfish imitation lures, called streamers on many fisheries in Cádiz. A hungry pike will grab anything in a flash on beautiful lakes in vicinity of Jaén's Sierra Cazorla national park. And Albacete and Cuenca are great places to catch barbel, brown and rainbow trout.

The more ambitious angler will be lured by the chance to catch wild brown trout from the River Trevélez, cascading off the Sierra Nevada's southern slopes, at 1,650 metres above sea level in the Alpujarra region of Granada.

My first impression of Spanish anglers, usually found in the local tackle shop is one of informality and friendliness. A few words of spoken Spanish will go a long way when interacting with fellow fishermen who, from my own experience are generous to a fault. Whether in offering to share lunch with a stranger by the river bank: or before they turn for home, by donating a proven fly lure that will entice hard to catch trout, as you persevere at dusk to catch your first fish, and they depart having caught nine.

Tackle shops are happy to sell you traditional fly fishing lures. A failsafe backup for fishermen in Spain is a brown sedge fly lure called a *pardón*.

Fly fishing is a comparatively recent development, so fly fishermen there are heavily influenced by English-language satellite TV fishing programs.

Spanish anglers have traditionally preferred to fish for the pot. Therefore by choosing to fish a catch and release stretch, often free fishing, anglers can frequently secure first rate fly fishing water in a stunning location and often all to themselves.

THE SMOOTH GUIDE TO FLY FISHING IN SOUTHERN SPAIN AND THE COSTA RESORTS

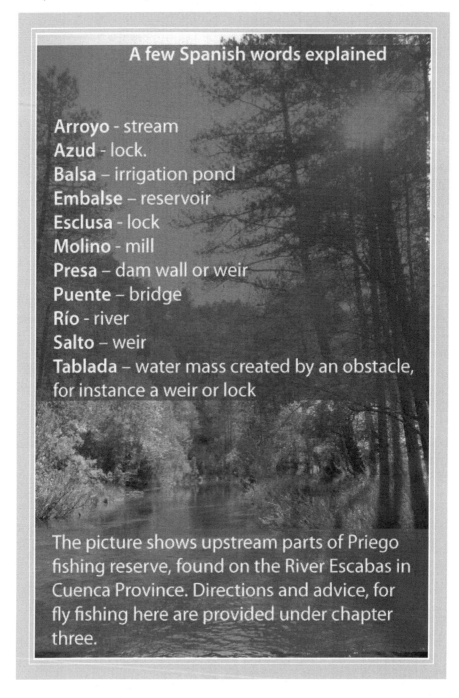

A few Spanish words explained

Arroyo - stream
Azud - lock.
Balsa – irrigation pond
Embalse – reservoir
Esclusa - lock
Molino - mill
Presa – dam wall or weir
Puente – bridge
Río - river
Salto – weir
Tablada – water mass created by an obstacle, for instance a weir or lock

The picture shows upstream parts of Priego fishing reserve, found on the River Escabas in Cuenca Province. Directions and advice, for fly fishing here are provided under chapter three.

Overview

CHAPTER ONE

THE SMOOTH GUIDE TO FLY FISHING IN SOUTHERN SPAIN AND THE
COSTA RESORTS

Practicalities

FISHING LICENCE AND RULES

Do I need a licence to fish in Spain?

Yes, it is a mandatory purchase. In general it can be obtained from any local office of the regional environment organisation, called Delegacion Agencia Medio Ambiente.

The price of a regional freshwater fishing licence (licencia de pesca fluvial) starts at €8 depending on where you fish. Anglers will need to take their passport or driving licence. The fishing licence covers an individual Spanish region for a minimum of one year and is valid for two rods. Anglers who are over sixty five years of age qualify for a free fishing licence valid for up to four years. Anglers under sixteen years old fish for free when accompanied by an adult in possession of a full fishing licence. Applicants can choose to secure a fishing licence that is valid for three or five years.

Details on where to purchase Spanish freshwater fishing licence are provided for each area mentioned in the guide book.

Remember that when you purchase a freshwater fishing licence, you should specify that you wish to fish for trout or salmon otherwise you may end up with just a freshwater, coarse fishing licence. Some Spanish regions require a small supplementary charge to your freshwater fishing licence if you intend to fish for trout or salmon.

Some regions require, in addition, the purchase of an insurance coupon; ask at the same time you purchase your freshwater fishing licence. In Andalucía for example the environment agency demands proof of an applicant's fishing proficiency in lieu of a fishing course and exam at the candidates own expense.

Anglers can order a freshwater fishing licence on-line. However the website goes on holiday in July and August. Cost is €15 plus €2 postage in Spain and by arrangement when ordering from U.K.

Visit: http://www.sulicencia.com/licenciapesca.htm#solicitarpesca

There are many kilometres of free fishing water available to anyone in possession of a freshwater fishing licence and these free fishing waters frequently maintain catch and release areas that are suitable for fly fishing.

The alternative to fishing free water is to pay to fish on a day ticket, fishing reserve (coto de pesca) further details are given in the next section. Fishing reserves contain the same fish species as free fishing water, for instance trout and occasionally salmon but are they're more intensively managed, some are catch and release others are subject to stocking.

Reservations for a fishing reserve can be made by purchasing a day ticket in advance from the Delegacion Agencia de Medio Ambiente (environment agency) present in the main towns and cities across Spain, or on the day, from local tackle shops, bars and restaurants. The average cost of a day ticket is €3 to €7.

Day tickets that aren't taken up in the annual pre-season ballot draw are made available for anglers to purchase during the fishing season from local outlets. Around 75% of day tickets are not taken up in Andalusia and València's pre-season ballot draws and so they're made available to anglers at local outlets during the season. Don't forget that in addition to day ticket fishing reserves, there are hundreds of kilometres of free fishing, catch and release rivers and lakes to enjoy.

Where can I go fishing?

Anglers new to fishing in Spain are often confused as to where and when they can and cannot fish. Put simply, freshwater fishing locations in Spain are divided between regulated and unregulated waters.

Regulated waters account for roughly 25% of all Spanish fisheries. All trout and salmon water (aguas trucheras y salmón) this includes rivers and reservoirs (embalses), are regulated by the government environment agency and they are clearly identified as such.

Regulated waters are split between free fishing, trout and salmon waters (zonas aguas libres declaradas trucheras) and areas controlled by special regulations of regional governments (zonas de régimen especial). These special zones contain day ticket, fishing reserves (cotos de pesca) that 95% of the times contain trout and salmon and always require purchase of a day ticket.

A bag limit is often imposed on the fishing reserves and a regular fishing season applies. These two types of water are increasingly nominated as catch and release areas (tramo pesca sin muerte). A minority of Spanish fishing reserves; about 5%, support coarse and sports fish populations, carp, American largemouth Black bass and barbel.

When a river or lake classed as unregulated, it means it doesn't fall into any of the above categories of water and this occurs roughly 75% of the time. Anglers may fish unregulated water for free and may stand a sporting chance of catching a trout but the water will usually support a greater proportion of coarse fish species.

On Spain's unregulated rivers and lakes anglers may fish all year through, usually a bag limit does not apply but some days are occasionally reserved for catch and release fishing, for instance in Castile and León region all fish species have to be returned alive on Monday and Thursday.
Readers are directed towards the author's book called The Essential Guide to Coarse Fishing in Spain that contains hundreds of excellent unregulated, free to fish Black bass, carp, pike, zander, pike and barbel waters that are suitable for fly fishing and spinning. The book is available via mail order from the author's webpage: www.spainfishing.com

The rules governing regulated waters are explained in further detail

Regulated, free fishing trout waters (zonas aguas libres declaradas trucheras) as opposed to unregulated free fishing waters are divided into two types of fishery and they are clearly signposted.

• Free fishing areas with traditional rules (zonas libres en régimen tradicional) allow a specified bag limit and the use of a wide range of specified baits.

• Free fishing waters that practice catch and release (zonas or tramos libres sin muerte) allow only artificial baits, fish must be returned alive and in good condition and only fly fishing or spinning with a single barbless hook is usually allowed. No day tickets are required to fish this type of water, anglers in possession of a freshwater fishing licence can turn up and cast.

Fisheries controlled by regional government's special regulations (zonas de régimen especial) they are divided into two parts.

• No fishing reserves (vedados de pesca) in which, temporarily or permanently, all fishing is prohibited or fishing for a particular species is banned.

• Secondly and of more significance for the angler fishing reserve (coto de pesca) where leisure angling is regulated in the interests of sustainable fish management. Permission needs to be obtained to fish here, usually in the form of a day ticket.

THE SMOOTH GUIDE TO FLY FISHING IN SOUTHERN SPAIN AND THE COSTA RESORTS

Fishing reserves are classed as follows:

• Intensive fishing reserve (coto de pesca intensivo) bag limit is allowed, periodic stocking is undertaken.

• Catch and release fishing reserve (coto de pesca sin muerte) all fish must be returned alive in good condition, maybe stocked.

• Normal fishing reserve with traditional regulations (coto de pesca en regimen tradicional) these reserves are not stocked but a bag limit usually applies.

• Fishing reserve managed jointly between a local fishing club and local government (escenario deportivo social / coto consorciado).

• Privately managed water (coto privado de pago) these fisheries are very few in number. Day tickets are needed to fish them and they may be purchased from a nearby town bar, failing that from the environment agency that also sells the angling licence.

A fishing reserve where a mix of coarse and game fishing takes place requires, in addition to the obligatory freshwater angling licence, a small supplementary charge for trout or salmon fishing: trout may only be caught from mixed species fishing reserves using artificial lures (includes fly fishing).

On these hybrid waters the fishing season for trout is from March 19th until August 31st in lowland water (aguas bajo montaña) and from May 14th until September 30th in uplands water (aguas alto montaña). Coarse angling is permitted year around every day and it's free fishing outside of the trout and salmon fishing season.

In water containing valuable fish types, special landscape or fauna that require special protection (zona de protección especial) is usually located near the source of mountain-rivers in national and natural parks.

Water that serves as a fish spawning ground (refugio de pesca), fishing is forbidden here.

Aquatic locations: where the gene pool of indigenous fish species and their biodiversity status are protected (reserva genética). Natural lakes (lagunas) they're few and far between in Spain, are frequently classified in this way in order to preserve their status as nature reserves for birdlife. Fishing may be vedado (banned) or a genetic reserve may occasionally be classed as catch and release free fishing stretch or area (zona pesca libre sin muerte) or a catch and release fishing reserve (coto e pesca sin muerte) see above for further explanation.

Fishing rules explained briefly

- Fishing reserves usually require a day ticket, unless thay are classed as free fishing, catch and release (tramo libre pesca sin muerte) and they are clearly sign posted. Day ticket fishing reserves are classed as follows:

- Intensive fishing reserve (coto de pesca intensivo) a bag limit is allowed, periodic stocking is undertaken.

- Catch and release fishing reserve (coto de pesca sin muerte) all fish must be returned alive in good condition.

- Normal fishing reserve with traditional angling regulations (coto de pesca en regimen tradicional) these reserves are not stocked, a bag limit applies.

- Fishing reserve managed jointly between a local angling club and the government (Escenario deportivo social or a coto consorciado).

- Privately managed day ticket fishery (coto privado de pago) these are very few in number. Day tickets are required to fish here and they may often be purchased from a nearby town bar, and failing that, from the environment agency, they also sell the fishing licence. (Refer to contents for a full account of Spain's fishing rules).

Andalusian barbel are caught from the river Huésnar, Seville

THE SMOOTH GUIDE TO FLY FISHING IN SOUTHERN SPAIN AND THE COSTA RESORTS

Tackle and Tactics

Size of rod will vary according to the size of your target fish and the distance you intend to cast. Line size: #3 up to #7

For rivers with dense bank side cover shorter rods will be more suitable. Line size: #3 - #5. Fishing the larger reservoirs you will require a longer rod for better control, 9'– 9 ½'. Line size: #6 or #7

Fishing from a boat in a reservoir for American largemouth Black bass, involves casting large, heavy baitfish imitation fly lures called poppers and streamers, size 4/0 – 8/0. Colours: gold, orange, yellow, silver, white and olive and black.

When fishing for coarse species, for instance carp use nymph lures' size 8-18 in similar colours to those lures that attract Black bass. For barbel use dry fly and nymph lures (bead heads) size 12-20, choose darker colours to imitate the hatch.

To attract trout on the surface or in shallow water, select a dry fly lure. A popular fly lure among Spanish trout anglers is a sedge lure (tricópteros). They will fish with a combination of nymph and dry fly often using a bubble plastic float (*buldo*), with a nymph fly lure attached to a second leader dropped off the mainline.

This fly lure presentation is more effective than using a single fly lure when fishing a *tablada* (water above a weir or other water obstacle) or a deeper pool (pozo - pronounced *poth-o*). Chest waders with felt sole bottoms or studs are essential here, especially at the start of the season when coldwater conditions are created by melt flow. English translations for popular Spanish fishing fly lure patterns are supplied in the appendix.

Fly fishing rules vary according to each Spanish region. A free annual booklet is available from the environment agency. In Andalusia you should ask for the 'Pesca Continental' booklet.

Ninety minutes drive south from Granada, the river Poqueira, high up in the Alpujarras (south facing Sierra Nevada) near the white village of Pampaneira provides visiting anglers with free fishing for brown trout.

THE SMOOTH GUIDE TO FLY FISHING IN SOUTHERN SPAIN AND THE COSTA RESORTS

Fly fishing for brown trout on the river Chulilla in València province.

THE SMOOTH GUIDE TO FLY FISHING IN SOUTHERN SPAIN AND THE COSTA RESORTS

An angler nets a brace of brown trout, from the river Turia. Waders are an advantage, where the water level changes during the day.

THE SMOOTH GUIDE TO FLY FISHING IN SOUTHERN SPAIN AND THE COSTA RESORTS

València

CHAPTER TWO

THE SMOOTH GUIDE TO FLY FISHING IN SOUTHERN SPAIN AND THE
COSTA RESORTS

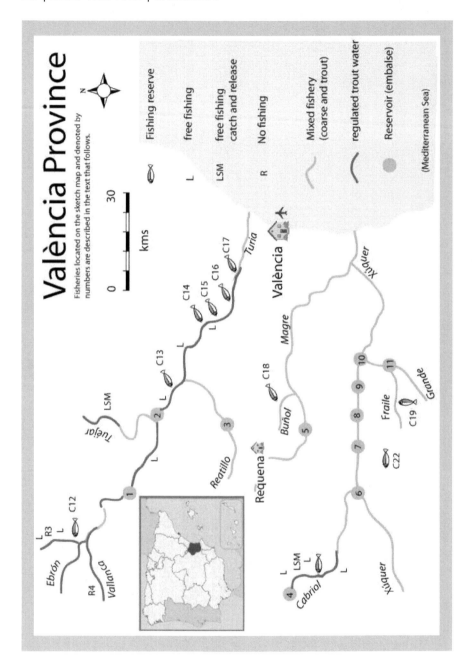

València

Fishing for brown trout on the river Chulilla, turn to page 26

Jan Morris in her book Spain states that "there are always fish about in Spain: fish in the stream beside the road....or - if they count as fish – those little wisps of elvers (baby eels) which are offered to you like dishes of some fine-spun pasta in every Valèncian eating house."

The major river is the Júcar (whose source is found in neighboring Castile-La Mancha region) and whose waters are depleted by extraction for irrigation in summer but replenish in spring and autumn when fishing is best. The smaller river Turia has its source in Turuel, found further north. Both rivers provide promising trout fishing opportunities.

Wild brown trout populations are found in the Ebrón, Vallanca, Palancia and Villahermosa Rivers.

Fishing licence and day tickets: Delegación Territorial de la Consellería de Agricultura y Medio Ambiente: Edificio Prop,
C/ Gregori Gea, 27. 46009 València
Tel, 963 86 62 59, 963 86 60 00. Or (012 - from Spain)

Rules

Comunidad Valènciana is an autonomous region of Spain, a single regional fishing licence covers the three provinces of València, Castellón and Alicante but not Murcia, this is a different region and requires a separate fishing licence

A fishing licence costs €8 for one year or €24 for three years. Anglers less than fourteen years old (when accompanied by a licence holding adult) and pensioners are exempt from payment.

Waters containing rainbow trout: fishing season runs from 21st March until 31st August. Fishing is permitted on free fishing stretches, not classified as catch and release, on Friday, Saturday, Sunday and public holidays using fly lures, spoon lures and artificial baits. On Tuesdays and Thursdays, which are not public holidays the same baits are permitted but only catch and release is allowed and barbless hook must be used.

Day tickets for fishing reserves

Trout fishing reserves, bag up: (Class 2) €10.10. Anglers over sixty-five years of age and under sixteen years old (Class 3) cost €5.10.

Catch and release and trout fishing reserves: (Class 3) €5.10. Anglers over sixty-five years of age and less than sixteen years old (Class 4), costs €2.5.

Ancient laws prohibited women from fishing at Marjal de Pego Lake near Oliva for five centuries, but in 2001 two successfully petitioned the regional government to reclaim their rights to supply València's restaurants with baby eels.

Brown trout caught from the river Chulilla

THE SMOOTH GUIDE TO FLY FISHING IN SOUTHERN SPAIN AND THE COSTA RESORTS

València's trout fisheries

Key

- Vedados (R) – forbidden to fish areas
- Acotado (C) – coto de pesca (fishing reserve)
- Aguas libres (L) – free fishing areas
- Aguas libres sin muerte (LSM) – free fishing, catch and release

A number follows each letter classification, and it denotes the order of fishing reserves (cotos de pesca), privately owned fishing reserves and free fishing areas shown on the provincial sketch map above and as contained in the free booklet called 'Temporada de Pesca' available from the environment agency.

River Cabriel: is a main tributary of the river Júcar and fishing starts below the main dam wall called 'presa de Mirasol' located above Contreras reservoir found near a bridge at Villatoya Bridge located at the crossroads of the N-332 between Requena and Albecete.

Coto La Terrera: river Cabriel, C11, brown trout, 2.2 km long. There are four other locations to fish along this reach, they are classified as: L, LSM, L & L – no day tickets are required. For information about outdoor activities visit: http://valledelcabriel.netai.net

River Ebrón: fishing commences where València province starts towards the confluence with the river Turia contains brown trout and a stretch classed as reserve R3.

River Vallanca: fish from river's source towards the confluence with the river Turia. Brown trout, this stretch contains a reserve classed as R4.

River Turia: fishing begins at Palanca Bridge, located upstream of the confluence of the Ebron with the Turia Rivers, towards a bridge found at Casas Altas.

The area contains **coto El Rincón de Ademuz** fishing reserve, river Turia, C12, catch and release, near to Ademuz town (rainbow trout, some brown trout). 4.2km long, 7m average channel width. It's an easy place to fish, there's not too much bank side vegetation. Day tickets are available from: the Hostal Domingo de Ademuz. No fishing on Tuesdays and Fridays. Directions: València west A-3 exit north at Utiel N-330 to Ademuz, which is just south of Rincón. The river offers alternative locations to fish, they are classified as: L, L.

River Turia: fishing starts from a lock called "azud de Cuevas Pedrera" by a dam signposted "La Presa" located upstream of El Marqués Bridge towards the Zagra Bridge. Rainbow trout, this stretch contains a reserve classed as R3L.

River Turia: fishing begins from the foot of the dam wall of Benagéber reservoir towards Riberas Bridge. Rainbow trout, this stretch contains two areas classed as LSM, L.

River Turia: fish from the foot of the dam called 'presa de Loriguilla' towards Paretotes until the downstream boundary of a fishing reserve called '**acotado de Ribarroja**'.

The river section also includes '**coto de Chulilla**', C13, catch and release fishing reserve, (brown and rainbow trout and barbel). Strong current with rapids, depth varies, 3.2km long. Local anglers' fish with a worm lure (*lombriz*) hook size number one and two: spoon and fly lures. Directions: València northwest CV-35 exit south at Losa Del Obispo for Chuililla.

'Acotado de Ribarroja' fishing reserve (River Turia)

El Rincón de Ademuz fishing reserve, on the river Turia

THE SMOOTH GUIDE TO FLY FISHING IN SOUTHERN SPAIN AND THE
COSTA RESORTS

The **river Chulilla** is a tributary of the river Turia, and it flows from north to south beginning below the floodgates of dam wall sign posted 'presa de Loriguilla' creating clear and cold water that is generally high in summer and low in winter due to excessive regulation. This is the opposite of what happens naturally.

The river follows a 10km course towards Chulilla, and there are three separate, contrasting fishing stretches along the way. The first stretch contains a meandering deep gorge called Hoces Del Turia. The river cuts through limestone cliffs called *cinglos*.

At the end of the first stretch the river Chulilla is diverted along a channel via 'presa Del Charco Azul' (blue pool). Crossing the town via a long tunnel to the power station sign posted 'Central Hidroeléctrica' located 4km along.

The second, canyon stretch is called 'tramo de las Hoces' it served for many years as a wild brown trout refuge due in part to its inaccessibility and fast current. But it also created some great fishing swims. Now days there is virtually no current from the blue pool to the power station, and many pools are filled with weeds or dried up. Both of these stretches are a shadow of their former trout fishing glory.

The third stretch starts at the exit to the power station and ends by the dam called 'presa Molina' where water is again diverted to a power station sign posted 'central de Gestalgar'. Along this stretch the river has regained its power and restored its fishing pools.

This third stretch contains **coto de Chulilla** (fishing reserve). It was never the best location for trout fishing, easily bettered by upstream parts. Presently this stretch is managed by a local fishing club called 'Pescadores de La Rinconá'. It has been stocked first with brown trout and then with rainbow trout.

Also found in the area is **coto de Villamarchante**, C16, catch and release stretch, Bugarra, (rainbow trout). It's shallow with many fish and 4.3 km long. Directions: València northwest CV-35 exit west at Liria CV-376 to Pedralba then onto Bugarra CV-377.

The river Chulilla between Bugarra and Gestalgar

THE SMOOTH GUIDE TO FLY FISHING IN SOUTHERN SPAIN AND THE COSTA RESORTS

There are six further locations to fish along this river reach, they are classified as: L, L, C14, L, C15 & C17.

1. **River Tuéjar**: fish from its source to the road bridge situated between València and Ademuz. Rainbow trout, this stretch contains a fishing reserve classed as catch and release fee fishing LSM.

2. **River Reatillo**: fish from: the ford called vado de La Aldobayo located upstream of the spring called "Fuente Santa Maria", until "Vado de la Hoya de Cherales". Rainbow trout, this stretch contains a free fishing reserve classed as L.

3. **River Reatillo**: fish from "Vado de la Hoya Cherales" until the confluence with river Turia, rainbow trout, stretch is classed as catch and release free fishing LSM.

4. **River Buñol**: fish from Carcalín Bridge towards the confluence with the river Chico. Stretch contains **coto La Jara** fishing reserve, rainbow trout, 3.5km long, C18.

5. **RIver Fraile**: fish from its source until the dyke called "Digue de la Molinera". Stretch contains **coto Fraile** fishing reserve, rainbow trout, 4.5km long, C19.

6. **River Vinalopó**: fish from its source until the lock house called "azud Casa de Monjas". Stretch includes **coto Vinalopó** fishing reserve, rainbow trout, 1.5km long, C20.

For the 2004 season, fishing was suspended on the river Ebrón from the Valèncian provincial border to the confluence with the river Turia. Fishing was also suspended on the river Vallanca from its source until the confluence with the river Turia. And on the river Júcar: in the town of Cullera along an 800m stretch. The bans may have been lifted by now. Please consult the free booklet called 'Temporada de Pesca' available from the environment agency (Medio Ambiente).

Barbel are frequently caught, using brown dry fly lures, from the River Villahermos near Castellón, page 31

THE SMOOTH GUIDE TO FLY FISHING IN SOUTHERN SPAIN AND THE COSTA RESORTS

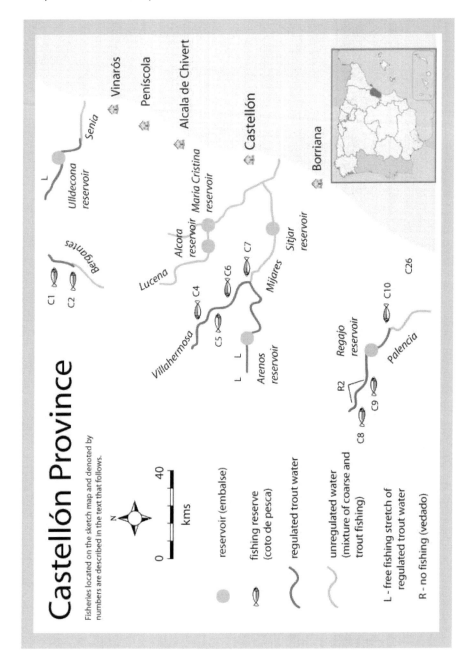

Castellón

Castellón has an over-achieving soccer team called Vila Real and many shoe factories. Hidden from view, but worthy of investigation are a good number of small rivers, which support productive trout fisheries flowing into the Mediterranean from nearby coastal ranges. They are found within ninety minute's drive, along good roads from either Reus (Tarragona) or València airports.

Fishing licence and day tickets: Conselleria de Medio Ambiente Servicio Territorial de Castellón. Avda. Hermanos Bou, 47 – 12003 Castellón de la Plana/ Castellón de la Planta Tel, 964 204211. Or 012 from Spain

Castellón's trout fisheries

River Bergantes: fish from the bathing area called fuente de Calinete or Los Baños until the boundary with Teruel province (Aragón region). This stretch supports rainbow trout and includes two day ticket fishing reserves, **coto Balma I**, C2, 3km long and **coto de Balma II**, C3, 4.3km long.

River Villahermosa: fish from the border of Castellón province to the road bridge connecting Argelita with Lucena, brown trout, R1. In 2004 no fishing was permitted along this stretch on coto Benagés, C4, 5 km long, **coto Cedramán**, C5, 2.8 km long and coto Ludiente, C6, 6 km long. The ban may have been lifted since then.

River Villahermosa: fish from the road bridge connecting Argelita with Lucena to the confluence with the river Mijares, rainbow trout. On this stretch is located **coto de Peñas Negras**, C7, see sketch map on next page, river Villahermosa, Argelita town, traditional fishing reserve (rainbow trout and barbel). This is a tributary of the river Mijares. The rainbow trout have acclimatized very well here and will readily take a dry fly lure. Some say that rainbow trout even reproduce here.

The water level goes down in summer. Contains many good size barbel that will take a fly lure. The downstream section is poor quality containing lots of riverweed and small trout. The best stretch is located at Argelita, where anglers take a path from the kiddies play area sign posted 'parque infatil' to the river at a point called fuente de Rapalo. Park up by the small esplanade found here and fish downstream. All types of golden-headed nymph fly lures and baitfish imitation fly lures called streamers work well

here. Also try dry fly lures like the red tag and butcher. Likewise large sedge fly lures size number twelve hook. Small mayfly lures are also worth trying.

The fishing reserve opens from the third Sunday in March until end of November. Seven bag limit and artificial fly lures only. Good access and a variety of different swims. Avoid August when it's too hot and full of mosquitoes. Nine anglers are permitted each day.

Day tickets: Bar Solsona de Ludiente, located 1km from Argelita. Anglers can buy a day ticket, a few days in advance, but only in person (offer to buy the proprietor a drink first) they don't accept reservations over the telephone. Apres pesca (after fishing) visit Bar La Calma located in Argelita where señora Teresa is renowned for her coffee and sandwiches.
 Description: 4.6km long, downstream stretch, fish from the road bridge that connects Argelita with Onda / Fanzara. The upstream stretch is located towards Ludiente arriving at a right turn for a bridge that crosses over the river. This bridge marks the upstream boundary of the fishing reserve. Cross over it to head downstream. Directions: north from València A-1/E-15 exit west at Nules CV-10 via Onda for Argelita. CV-20 80km distance

River Mijares: fish from Castellón province boundary until the power station dam, signposted 'presa hidroeléctrica de Montanejos'. Rainbow trout, this river section contains a stretch classed as free fishing L.

River Mijares: fish from Arañuel town square, called 'Casilla de Camineros' until Cámping de Cirat. Rainbow trout, this river section contains a stretch classed as free fishing L.

River Palencia: fish from the boundary of Navajas with Segorbe until Castellnovo Bridge. This stretch includes **coto Segorbe**, C10 it contains rainbow trout. Fishing was suspended in 2004 on coto de Teresa, C9 4.2 km long, and **coto de Bejís**, C8, 3.1 km long, the ban may have been lifted since then, please consult with the environment agency, contact details are given at the start of this chapter.

River Sénia: fish from water guage station (estación de aforos), located downstream of the dam, presa de Uldecona until the Tarragona provincial boundary (Catalonia). Rainbow trout, this river contains a stretch classed as free fishing L.

Coto Els Estanys and La Ponderosa (28ha): otherwise known as Lagunas de Almenara, carp and barbel. Directions: València due north exit N-340 at Almenara.

River Mijares

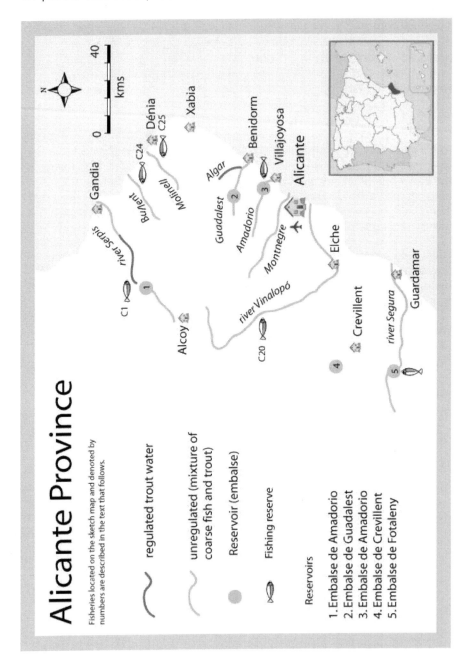

Alicante Province

Fisheries located on the sketch map and denoted by numbers are described in the text that follows.

regulated trout water

unregulated (mixture of coarse fish and trout)

Reservoir (embalse)

Fishing reserve

Reservoirs

1. Embalse de Amadorio
2. Embalse de Guadalest
3. Embalse de Amadorio
4. Embalse de Crevillent
5. Embalse de Fotaleny

Alicante

Middle reaches, of the river Serpis near l'Orxa; showing a high water level

The Segura is Alicante's main river (whose source is found in Andalusia – to the south west) and there are smaller rivers in the area, for instance the Vinalopó, which are usually short, and have little current (due to agricultural usage, climatic reasons or both) and frequently completely dry during the summer but offer good fishing opportunities outside this time..

Fishing licence and day tickets: Delegacion de Agricultura y Medio Ambiente, Edificio Prop, C/Churruca, 29, 03071 Alicante Tel: 965 900600. Or 012 from Spain

Coto de Beniarrés, C1, river Serpis, day ticket required, catch and release, L'Orxa, (rainbow trout and barbel) stocked eight times each season with trout. A small river: with a lot of clear deep pools. A local fishing club, called Sociedad de Pescadores Deportivos de Alcoy, is responsible for the management of the fishing reserve.

Bigger fish up to 40cm in length are caught downstream of the lock. Catch and release on Monday, Thursday and Friday: weekends have a six bag limit 21cm minimum size.

Water quality and current is good upstream by Alcoy thanks to the contribution of tributaries for instance the river Algar. Below the dam fishing is fine and not affected unduly by releases from the reservoir. Although after a day spent wading in the river the mud on your boots washed downstream from the reservoir's sediment will stink a bit. Day tickets: Bar Del Polideportivo in L'Orxa.

Description: 6.5km long. The fishing reserve is located downstream of Beniarres reservoir. Fish (officially): from L'Orxa Bridge until Villalonga. But in practice, fish from the first railway tunnel that runs parallel with the river for the next 3km approximately. Directions: from Alicante north N-340 exit east at Benimarfull northeast CV-705 to L'Orxa. See sketch map opposite.

In 2004 fishing was banned on the river Algar from its source to the confluence with the river Guadalest and on a river called 'Barranco de la Encantada' from its source to the confluence with the river Serpis. The ban may have been lifted since then. Consult with the environment agency for further for details.

Cotos de Bullent, Molinell, Amadorio and Fortaleny (fishing reserves) are coarse fishing reserves, a day ticket is required,. Information about these waters is given in my book called The Essential Guide to Coarse Fishing in Spain. For further information see end of this book or visit the author's webpage: www.spainfishing.com

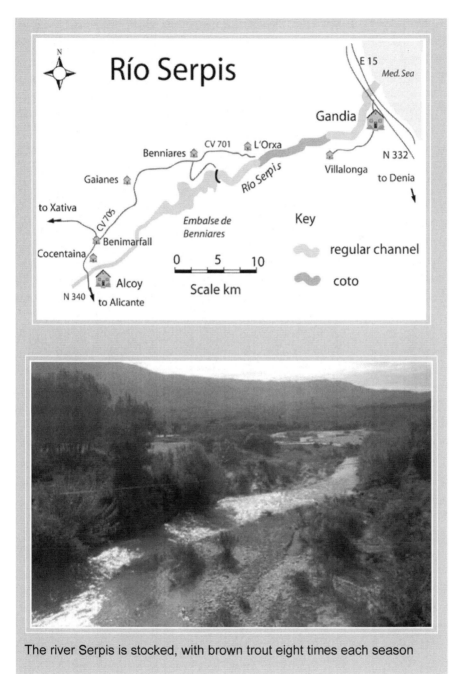

The river Serpis is stocked, with brown trout eight times each season

Imitation black ant lures are favoured by anglers, who aim to bag a trout or barbel from Murcia's fisheries

Murcia

CHAPTER THREE

THE SMOOTH GUIDE TO FLY FISHING IN SOUTHERN SPAIN AND THE
COSTA RESORTS

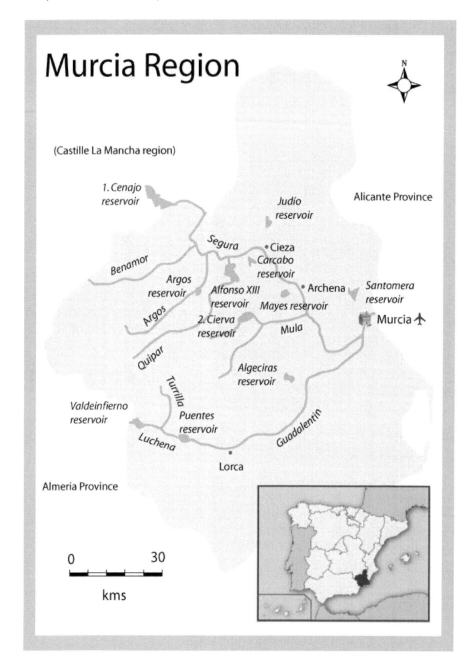

Murcia Region

(Castille La Mancha region)

Alicante Province

1. Cenajo reservoir

Judío reservoir

Segura

Cieza

Benamor

Carcabo reservoir

Argos reservoir

Alfonso XIII reservoir

Archena

Santomera reservoir

Argos

Mayes reservoir

Murcia

2. Cierva reservoir

Mula

Quipar

Algeciras reservoir

Turrilla

Valdeinfierno reservoir

Puentes reservoir

Guadalentín

Luchena

Lorca

Almeria Province

0   30

kms

Murcia

A beautiful brown trout, caught from the river Segura

Murcia has booming tourist developments which take advantage of the mild weather and sandy beaches. Murcia experiences up to one hundred and fifty days in the year where the sky is totally clear. At this time some visitors take the opportunity to explore excellent wineries that have been developed near the towns of Bullas, Yecla and Jumilla.

April and October are the months with the most rain, there being frequent heavy downpours in a single day. At this time anglers choose to go fishing in nearby rivers and lakes.

Fishing licence and day tickets: Dirección General Del Medio, Oficina de Caza y Pesca, Catedrático Eugenio Úbeda Moreno, 3. CP 30008 Murcia. Tel, 968 228913/14/15 and 968 362628 & 968 283918 E-mail address: cazaypesca@carm.es

Rules: minimum bag size for rainbow trout is 19cm. Anglers can fish with up to three fly lures when employing a bubble float. No fishing is allowed in ditches and irrigation canals beside the rivers except when they're classified as coarse fishing water. No fishing is allowed within 50m of dam walls and entrance and exits to fish passes. No live baiting. Ten bag limit for rainbow trout unless stated otherwise.

Murcia's trout fisheries

1. **Coto de El Cenajo**, river Segura, day ticket required, part time intensive fishing reserve, Salmerón (rainbow trout and barbel) stretch is 8km long. Fish from a dam wall called Presa Del Cenajo downstream until Casa Del Hondón.

Fishing is permitted all year every day but from 1st June until 15th October the river stretch is classed as a fishing reserve when it's open on Thursday, Saturday, Sunday and on public holidays. From 8am until 3pm. Ten bag limit for trout but no bag limit for barbel. Minimum size is 19cm for trout and 18cm for barbel.

Forty anglers are permitted each day. Closed during the summer when the river is diverted for irrigation. Directions: from Murcia head northeast N-301 exit west on C-3314 to Calasparra. Now take local roads to the stretch.

2. **Coto de Embalse de la Cierva**, Cierva reservoir, day ticket required, part time intensive fishing reserve managed by a fishing club, Mula (rainbow trout, common carp and some other coarse fish species, barbel, Black bass). For local advice and day tickets contact: fishing club Asociación Deportiva de Pescadores de Mula.

The fishing reserve has 6.3km of bank to cast from covering the whole reservoir. Anglers are not allowed to fish within 150m of the dam wall. Classed as a fishing reserve from 1st June until 31st October when it's open on Thursday, Saturday, Sunday and public holiday. Outside this period it's open all year everyday. Bag limit is seven trout, ten fish for all other species. Twelve anglers are permitted on Thursdays, otherwise twenty five, and thirty five on public holidays. Directions: Murcia east C-415 to Mula Judío.

El Cenajo fishing reserve, on the river Segura at Almadenes canyon

THE SMOOTH GUIDE TO FLY FISHING IN SOUTHERN SPAIN AND THE
COSTA RESORTS

Cierva reservoir

3. **Coto El Esparragal**, river Segura, day ticket required, part time intensive fishing reserve managed by a fishing club, Calasparra (trout, barbel) stretch is 2km long from dam wall called 'presa de El Esparragal' to the final part of the irrigation channel that joins with the river Segura. There is a no-fishing zone that runs for 740m from Cortijo Del Macaneo. Fishing is allowed all year every day but the water is classed as a fishing reserve from 31st March until 3rd November when it's open on Thursdays Saturday, Sunday and public holidays from 8 am until 2 pm. Bag limit is seven trout.

Fifty anglers are permitted each day. Day tickets are available locally from Asociación de Pesca Calasparra, C/ Ordonez, 34, Bajo.30420, Calasparra-Murcia. Local anglers recommend good fishing swims from downstream of the weir at the Central Eléctrica until a few kilometres upstream of cueva de los Monigotes with the fishing reserve. Directions: from Murcia head northeast N-301 exit west on C-3314 to Calasparra.

River Segura

4. **Coto Hoya García**, river Segura, day ticket required, intensive fishing reserve managed by angling club, Cieza (trout) fish from Azud de Hoya García until the Central Hidroelétrica del Progreso: in other words from the lock to the power station. Season runs from 15th May until 15th September on Wednesday, weekends and public holidays. Fish from: 8 am until 3 pm. After 3pm it's catch and release only. There is a seven bag limit for trout. Forty anglers are permitted each day. Day tickets are available locally from the Asociacíon de Pesca Fluvial Ciezana Del Segura. Directions: from Murcia head northwest N 301 exit west for Cieza C 330.

5. **Coto El Jarral**, river Segura, day ticket required, intensive fishing reserve managed by angling club, Abarán (trout). Fish from Abarán old bridge (puente viejo de Abarán) until100m downstream of Central Hidroeléctrica Nicolás, in other words from: the old bridge at Abarán to just below a power station. Fish from: 31st May until 15th September on Tuesday, Friday, weekends and public holidays. From 8 am till 3 pm. There is a seven bag limit for trout and forty anglers are permitted to fish each day. Day tickets can be purchased from the local angling club called Sociedad Aberanera de Pescadores. Directions: from Murcia head northwest N 301 exit west for Abarán MU 402.

The following rivers and reservoirs (man made lake) are fee to fish and there is no bag limit. They are un-stocked but trout will often be found, sharing water with barbel and carp.

- River Luchena situated near Lorca, and Mula. Both rivers may be fished along their entire length all year round and every day. No fishing is allowed on the Quípar and Argos rivers situated near Cehegin and the river Benamor situated near Moratalla.

- Embalse de Argos has 12km of shoreline to fish and is situated near Cehegin anglers can't fish at the entrance of the river into the reservoir from February till August to protect spawning grounds. Elsewhere fishing is allowed all year.

- Embalse Alfonso XIII has 17km of shoreline to fish and is situated near Calasparra anglers can't fish at the entrance of the river into the reservoir from Febuary till August. Elsewhere fishing is allowed all year.

- Embalse Del Cárcabo situated near Cieza fishing is allowed all year every day.

- Embalse de Algeciras situated near Alhama de Murcia fishing is allowed all year every day.

- Embalse Del Judio has 8.3km of shoreline to fish and is situated near Cieza fishing is allowed all year every day.

- Embalse Del Mayés has 2km of shoreline to fish and is situated near Ojós fishing is allowed all year every day.

- Embalse de Puentes situated near Lorca fishing is allowed all year every day.

- Embalse Azud de Ojós has 7.9km of shoreline to fish and is situated near Blanca fishing is allowed all year every day. No fishing is allowed at Embalse Santomera situated near Fortuna.

River Segura near Archena, refer to Murcia sketch map found on page 40.

THE SMOOTH GUIDE TO FLY FISHING IN SOUTHERN SPAIN AND THE COSTA RESORTS

Puente Ortega fishing reserve, on the river Guadalquiver, in Jaén province, turn to page 115

THE SMOOTH GUIDE TO FLY FISHING IN SOUTHERN SPAIN AND THE COSTA RESORTS

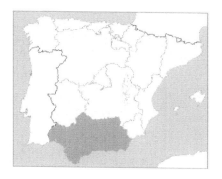

Andalusia

CHAPTER FOUR

THE SMOOTH GUIDE TO FLY FISHING IN SOUTHERN SPAIN AND THE
COSTA RESORTS

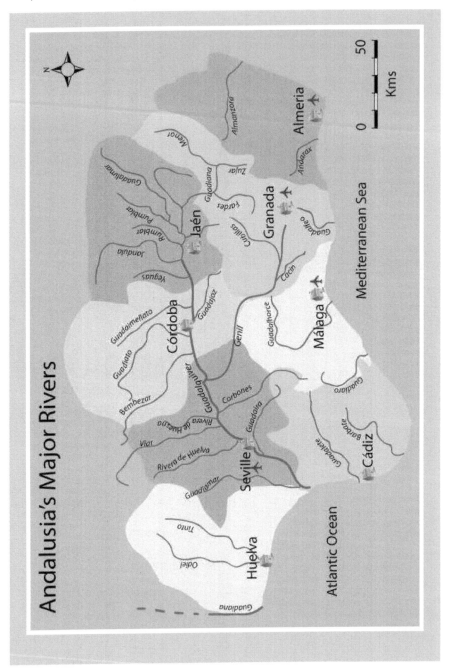

Andalusia

Downstream section of the river Treveléz in Granada province,
turn to page 90 for directions and advice on tackle and tactics

Visitors can escape Andalusia's lowland interior, a frying pan during the
summer months, by venturing into the cooler highlands surrounding Jaén
and Granada and anglers can look forward, to a fantastic time fly fishing in
wonderful rivers and lakes.

In Jaén province, amongst the wonderful natural parks of Sierra de Cazorla,
Segura and Las Villas are found wonderful trout rivers like the Borosa,
Guadalquiver, Segura and Madera. Also in the mix are mountain trout
streams found in Granada's Alpujarras region (on the southern slopes of
Sierra Nevada), the Genil and Trevélez Rivers.

Fisheries are signposted

Rules

In general the season for free trout-fishing waters is divided between lowlands and mountain areas. High mountain waters (sign posted 'aguas de alta montaña' - mountain streams and reservoirs where the trout fishing season is shorter than elsewhere in Spain) the fishing season runs from the second Sunday in May until 30th September.

And low mountain waters (sign posted 'aguas baja montaña') where the fishing season runs from the last Sunday in March until 31st August and is extended into September and October, in many instances for catch and release fishing.

Fishing on free fishing, trout waters is allowed every day except non-festive Mondays, when stockings take place. Fishing times vary according to individual fishing reserves, which are mentioned under separate provincial headings.

In free fishing waters (sign posted 'aguas pesca libre') the bag limit is ten rainbow trout, per angler per day: remember that brown trout must be returned immediately to the water because they're considered an endangered species in Andalusia. The minimum size for rainbow trout is 19 cm. Black bass is 21cm in water classed as catch and release (sign posted 'aguas pesca sin muerte').

All the rivers and reservoirs, mentioned below under separate provincial headings, are classed as trout fishing fisheries (sign posted 'aguas trucheras'). In addition there are no-fishing areas (sign posted 'refugios de pesca') for instance, spawning grounds, and privately owned fishing reserves (sign posted 'acotodas de pesca'), not many exist in Spain because land is put to more profitable use for hunting, signposted 'coto de caza'. Rivers and reservoirs that do not fall into these two categories can still be fished but are recognised as mixed fisheries (a mixture of coarse and trout fishing) where trout may occasionally be caught but as a rule are not present in such large numbers.

Best times to go fishing

The fishing season starts later in the higher altitude streams of the Sierra Nevada and Sierra de Grazalema in order to allow cold melt water to pass, the best time to fish here is in late May or early June.

High mountain areas (sign posted 'ríos de alto montaña') are narrow and fast flowing in general. Where dense bank side cover is present; short bow casts, lateral casts and roll casts, less than seven metres in distance are the order of the day. Try striking sideways under these conditions.

Smaller, upland streams may experience low water levels in late summer. By September lowland dammed rivers, for instance the river Huéznar, located north of Seville, will experience their highest levels as water is accumulated over the course of a fishing season, which builds up behind dams.

Larger fish hold up by waterfalls and in deeper pools in lowland water, anglers fish for larger specimens using streamers (baitfish imitation feather lures) and small minnow imitation lures. Select an 8 ½ ' rod with a medium or slow action to aid bow casts, line #2 #3 or #4.

Andalusia fishing licence

This is a mandatory purchase for fishing in Andalucía. Visit any, Consejería de Medio Ambiente (environment agency office). And these offices are listed under separate provincial headings.

A freshwater Andalusia fishing licence costs €5.54 for one year, €16.62 for three years and €27.69 for five years. A trout fishing supplement costs €2.75 for one year, €8.26 for three years and €12.65 for five years. An Andalusia fishing licence that includes trout fishing and the licence is classed as: Categoria – ABSOLUTA. A boat surcharge costs €5.54 for oars only for one year and €11.07 for a boat with a motor.

Anglers less than sixteen years old fish for free when accompanied by a licence holding adult. Anglers over sixty five years old can also request a free fishing licence.

Affiliated banks that are authorised to receive payment on behalf of the environment agency for the regional angling licence include CajaMar, Caja Rural de Granada, Caja Rural de Córdoba, Caja Rural de Jaén, Caja Rural del Sur (Seville and Huelva), Banco de Andalucía, Tel, 902 301 000, Banco Popular Español, Tel, 902 301 000. Further information is provided at the end of the guide book.

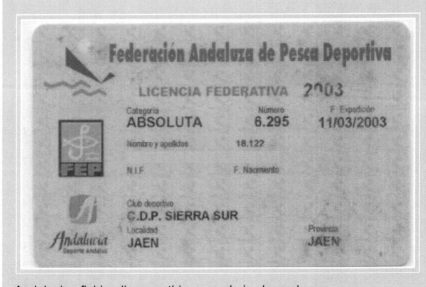

Andalusian fishing licence, this example is classed as Categoria-ABSOLUTA, which allows the holder to fish for trout

Andalusia fishing licence explained in further detail
Hundreds of stories are told every year, by frustrated anglers, who have encountered bureaucratic difficulties when attempting to obtain Andalusía's freshwater fishing licence. On their part, the Spanish environment agency says that they issue 60,000 fishing licences annually and that 150,000 fishing licences are in present circulation.

On 20th January 2003 the Andalusia environment agency installed a new computer system to handle fishing licence applications. The agency' computer allegedly cannot distinguish between applications for hunting and fishing licences and therefore applicants who are unable to prove proficiency, a good thing for those intending to use a gun on public land, are required to undertake an official three-day training course followed by an exam.

The Andalusia government charges €50.33 for a fishing course and €25.17 to take the obligatory exam. Successful candidates receive their regional fishing licence six months later. Questions, included in the infamous fishing exam, are available to download from the author's webpage www.spainfishing.com

A free fisherman's handbook containing advice on how to pass the Andalusia fishing licence exam, called Manuel Del Pescado, is available from 'Mailing Andalucía', Tel, 95 423 7040 / 95 423 6863.

The easiest way to by-pass this procedure is to present a UK or Spanish fishing licence, from any Spanish province, valid between 5th January 1991 and 5th January 1995. Exemptions from the fishing exam are provided for holders of a fishing licence for any two years out of the previous five.

In this case the fishing licence can then be obtained by presenting duplicate copies of your passport (Spanish residents will bring two copies of a *residencia* (letter of residence), photocopied both sides and obtained from the town hall.

Angling insurance, to cover public liability, is now mandatory and this too must be obtained when seeking a fishing licence; the policy number on your Spanish household insurance will cover this procedure.

Reasonably priced day tickets for fishing reserves can also be purchased on the day locally from the Agente forestall (natural park's office) located in the vicinity of a fishing reserve and from local restaurants and bars.

A booklet is published annually by the Andalusia government called 'Pesca Continental en Andalucía'. Email the environment agency for a free copy.

For further information contact: Direccíon General de Gestíon del Medio Natural, Avda. Manuel Siurot, 50. 41071 Sevilla.
Tel, 955 00 34 00. E-mail address: cazaypesca.cma@juntadeandalucia.es
Webpage address: www.juntadeandalucia.es/medioambiente

If anglers experience a problem applying for a fishing licence they're directed by the Andalusia government to call free phone: 900 850 500 between 8 a.m. and 9 p.m.

To organise a fishing licence on-line go to webpage address:
www.juntadeandalucia.es/medioambiente/cazaypesca/licencias.html

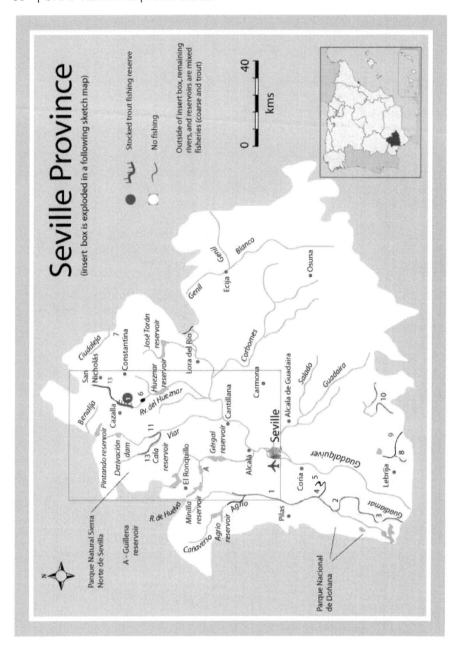

Seville

Seville is one of the hottest parts of Spain although its winters are generally mild. Maximum temperatures in summer often surpass 40°C. During the summer vacation, Seville's inhabitants escape the oppressive city heat by vacating to the north, where natural parks, containing rivers and lakes allow visitors to take in beautiful surroundings and go fishing.

Fishing licence and day tickets: Delegación Provincial de Medio Ambiente: Avda. Innovación, s/n, Poligono Aeropuerto 41071. Seville. Tel, 955 00 44 00, fax, 955 004489.
E-mail address: Delagada.se.cma@juntadeandalucia.es

Seville's trout and barbel fisheries

Molino Del Corcho fishing reserve is located along the River Huéznar near to Estación de Cazalla and Constantina, approximately 1½ hours drive north from Seville. Visitors can also take the train. This is a summer holiday destination and the big attractions are beautiful scenery and good fishing. There is a wide choice of accommodation available near rivers that have easy access from the train station via local taxi, bus or bike.

A number precedes a fishing location, mentioned further below and this number is also found, in a red circle, on the Seville provincial map shown immediately below. But you will also find further fisheries included on the more detailed insert map, shown on next page.

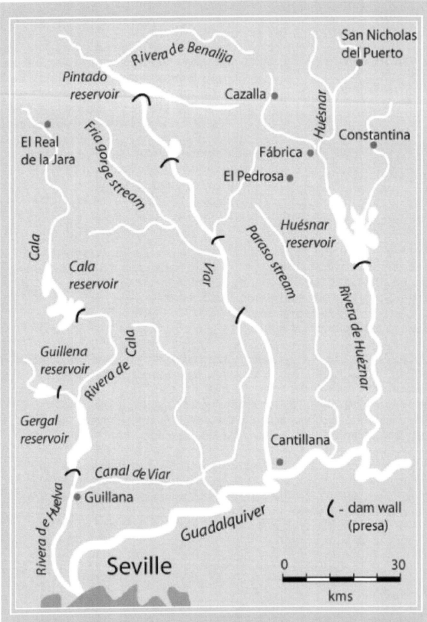

Insert box, exploded from Seville province sketch map found on page 56

THE SMOOTH GUIDE TO FLY FISHING IN SOUTHERN SPAIN AND THE COSTA RESORTS

1. **Coto de Molino del Corcho**, River Huésnar, day ticket
required, intensive fishing reserve rules apply, Cazalla and Constantina
(rainbow trout and barbel) barbel spawn in upstream areas. Fly and
spinning lures only are allowed, ten bag limit, minimum size is 19cm. Ten
anglers are permitted to fish everyday, all year except non-festive Mondays,
Tuesday and Wednesday, and thirty anglers on weekends and public
holidays. Keep an eye out for the family of otters. This is a pretty location to
fish at.

Try using a pheasant tail imitation fly lure with a gold body (cola de faisan
torax dorado). A sedge fly lure with red deer hair works well. Imitation
nymphs to use include olive, brown and yellow (olivas, tabacos and
amarilla). Dry fly lures include cream or brown emergent mayfly (efimeras
del marrón al crema) black midge fly lures (dípteros negros) and small
sedge fly lures in chestnut or brown (pequeños tricopteros marrones y
pardos – good at the start of the trout fishing season in March and April).

Day tickets: the environment agency office located in Isla Margerita 800m
upstream from the C 432 road bridge is found downstream of Rivera Del
Huéznar. Day tickets are also available from the natural park's office:
Oficina Del Parque Natural Sierra Norte, Constantina Tel, 955 88 12 26.
And from: Camping de la Fundición de Plata located on the road to San
Nicolás del Puerto, next to the River Huéznar, Tel, 955 954117.

Description: the fishing reserve is 10km long, fish from the road bridge
connecting Cazalla de la Sierra with Constantina downstream until the exit
of Cortijo de Jesús gulley. Directions: Seville go north C-433 to El Pedroso.
Now take local roads to the river stretch. The river runs parallel to the road
SE-168 road heading towards San Nicholas, this road begins a the junction
with the A-455 road connecting Constantina with Cazalla. The fishing
reserve is located 7km from Constantina.

The insert box sketch map, shown above, presents locations for the
fisheries that are mentioned below. The following waters are free fishing
areas that often contain trout, except for a reservoir sign posted 'embalse
de Gergal'.

• Garganta de las Gateras: gulley – north part, Sierra Norte de Sevilla
• Garganta de las Gateras: gulley – south party, Sierra Norte de Sevilla
• Rivera de Cala, south part.
• River Viar: fish a ford sign posted 'vado de las Gateras'.
• Rivera de Benalija: Hoya de Btra Sra, Cuevas de Santiago.
• River Huéznar, fish a ford sign posted 'vado en la Jarosa'.
• River Huéznar: fish the rapids stretch.

Récula de Cantra Lobos is a sluice, free fishing, embalse de Gergal, Rivera de Huelva. Directions: from Seville go north, exit at Glorieta de San Lázar SE-30 sign posted "barriada de San Jerónimo". Past a cemetery wall, traffic lights are to the left, at the crossroads by the church, heading towards Algaba A-431. After a while head towards Alcalá de Río. Before Alcalá, take a left turn SE-188 towards Torre de la Reina (a further 3km). Having passed through this town, after 5km, at the crossroads take the A-460 (Guillena - Burguillos) left turn to Guillena and 1km on is the bridge over Rivera de Huelva. And then immediately: the entrance to Guillena, 300m on from the bridge on the same road at the start of right along a service canal for the EMASESA water company. 2km along the channel is a locked iron gate: with a notice board "coto de Caza" (hunting reserve) and another sign "Granado suelto" indicating presence of El Torro Bravo (fighting bulls).

300m on from the bridge on the same road at the start of town 100m on at the traffic lights take a right turn onto the SE-187 road, head towards los Pajanosas. After 3km, cross the bridge over the Regato El Sardinero where a small track leads from the Park up here and walk downstream towards the récula de Cantalobos (sluice gate) it corresponds with the stream of the same name that joins up with river Huelva, for a ravine that passes just to the right of an iron gate.

2km from the iron gate, access is provided to the bottom of the sluice, to the stretch where Cantalobos stream enters the reservoir. Take the track that circles to the left of a slight incline, take a lane to the right that descends to the meadow until arriving at the small reservoir, sign posted 'pantano'. There is a steep incline at the end of the route. And you have to cross over a wire fence. And a notice that requests you not to make the climb since there is livestock loose in the vicinity, dark chestnut bulls which may give an unforgettable shock.

Instead visitors may prefer to take the car outside of the land owned by livestock breeders. After passing the iron-gate, in order to fish the lake on land managed by EMASESA contact Senor Gerente of the town council at: calle Escaules Pías, no 2, de Sevilla for written permission. His permission is easy to obtain. In addition take along your driving licence and a passport in case you bump into the Guardia Civil on the fishing bank.

Andalusian barbel are caught from the river Huésnar

River Huéznar, good swim found by a mill called Molino Del Castraño, Rivera de Huéznar, contains large Andalusia barbel, also known as Gypsy barbel, they are present all through this river system and they are called *barbo Gitano* in Spain. Even larger Comiza barbel exist in just a few locations, mainly in the **tail end of Huéznar reservoir**, barbel enter reservoirs during the summer and return to rivers to spawn, and upper reaches of **Rivera Del Huéznar**, they will often take a popper or streamer, baitfish imitation fly lure or a spinning lure, in summer from the reservoir. Comiza barbel are extinct in the lower reaches of the river Guadalquiver. Carp will find their way upstream to **zona Del Molino del Castaño**. American largemouth Black bass can be caught from embalse de Huéznar towards the area called **zona de Fábrica**. They are usually small. Cachuelo (Pyrennean chub) are caught upstream of zona de Fábrica.

Occasionally rainbow trout are caught here but are more often found from the intensive fishing reserve. Brown trout are caught further upstream. Alevines (trout fry) under 5cm long, called, are present in **zona de La Umbria**.

Directions: from Seville head northeast C-433 via San Jerónimo to Alcalá de Río Cantillana then A-431 for Cantillana. From here follow signs for Sierra Norte towards El Pedroso and Cazalla de la Sierra. A-432.

Digressing slightly, 11km from Cantillana A-432, you will encounter a good access route for the **river Viar**, to the left on a sealed track over a barrier that takes agricultural machinery. A little further up the A-432 is a turn for Castillblanco de los Arroyos C-433 and along here is found **zona de Melonares** where inevitably a new dam is being built that will destroy this virgin forest river channel. A bridge over the river Viar is located 5km ahead.

From Pedroso take crossroads towards Cazalla. 5km ahead is a right turn for Constantina A-452. At this point: there are number of ways to proceed. You may continue on the A-432 towards Fabrica de El Podroso. Or go via Contantina on the A-452 if you want to gain access to the tail end of embalse de **Huéznar reservoir**, where you stand a good chance of catching barbel in summer. Down a track called La Umbria where you can park up. A further 150m ahead is the foot of the river. From here you can venture upstream towards **zona Militar** or go downstream along a pretty path towards a water mill river stretch called **zona Del Molino del Castaño**.

The water level here is good, fishing in the lovely **San Pedro stream** there are channel obstacles for the barbel to negotiate in the fierce current, upstream to the exit of an old mill. Further upstream, look for a track that goes past an old empty railway station in Fábrica. This track goes to the right of the road to Cazalla A-432 then switches back towards the old military installations of Fábrica. And passes downstream of the section of San Pedro stream, where barbel migrate upstream in order to spawn.

A further 200m upstream there is an uphill halt. From here you can take the car or follow on foot the train track until you cross the railway bridge over the river. Over the bridge you can go left or right for the river. This is a very remote area, take a friend for company. Finally, to access **zona de La Jarosa** - downstream stretch and tail end of the reservoir, head towards Constantina to the fork of the A-432 andd A-452 roads. 1km on the right take the entrance to zona Recreativa and Futuro Camping, sign posted "canadiense". Go over the cattle grid and park up by the barbeque area. The river is a few metres ahead.

Andalusian barbel are caught from the river Viar

River Viar, Tabla de Vado de las Perillas – weir pool, directions: from Seville head northeast A-431 past Alcalá Del Río towards Lora Del Río. Exit before hand at Cantillana. Now pass a bridge over the river Viar. After the bridge you will pass a service station, a restaurant – sign posted 'venta', on your right and an asphalted stretch of road. There after the condition of the road deteriorates, so take hold. After a further 6km park up next to a closed iron gate: (or proceed if driving an SUV). To the right of the gate leaves a lane that you proceed along to the ford, located 200m downstream. Upstream or downstream is equally good to fish.

• River Viar: rapids at Vado de las Perillas.
• River Viar: rapids at Vado de las Perillas.
• Embalse de El Gergal, Récula de Contalobos - sluice gate.

Migrant ascent of barbel takes place annually in **Rivera de Benalija** upstream: towards Cuevas de Santiago found near Cazalla de la Sierra.

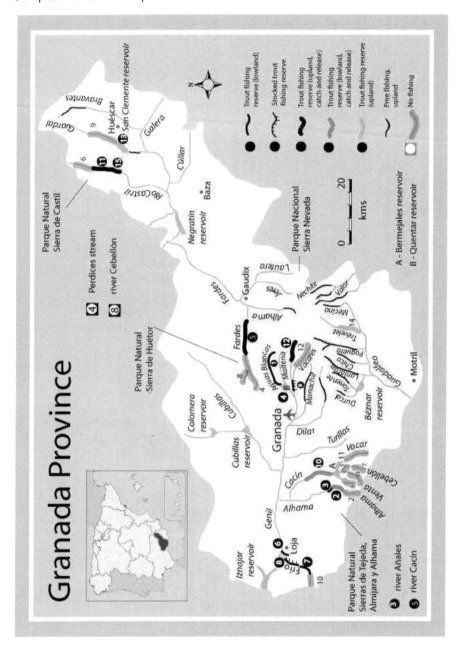

THE SMOOTH GUIDE TO FLY FISHING IN SOUTHERN SPAIN AND THE
COSTA RESORTS

Granada

Alhama fishing reserve, on the river Alhama

Although slightly too far east to catch the floods of holidaymakers coming to the Costa del Sol via Málaga, Granada brings in a number of tourists with its Moorish architecture, including the famous Alhambra palace (the view at sunset from the old quarter of the city is quite something). Granada too has many productive rivers that contain wild brown trout, which by law must be returned safely to the water, and stocked rainbow trout that grow big in nearby man made lakes, signposted 'embalse' (reservoir) or 'presa' (dam wall).

The city of Granada is a great place to make your base. Local bars serve generous, free *tapas* with each beer of glass or wine ordered – we ate for 'free' during our four day stay.

Fishing licence and day tickets: Delegación Provincial del Medio Ambiente: C/Marqués de la Ensenada, 1. s/n. 18071. Granada. Tel: 958 02 60 00.Fax; 958 02 60 58. E-mail: address Delegado.gr.cma@juntadeandalucia.es

Granada's trout fisheries

1. **Coto de Aguas Blancas**, river Aguas Blancas, day ticket required, low mountain-water rules apply, Quéntar (rainbow trout and barbel) is a tributary of the river Genil. This is a narrow channel with dense bank side cover. The fishing reserve is 10km long alternating between wide glides and deeper pools with a few riffle sections. Artificial baits only. Ten bag limit. Minimum size is 19cm. Ten anglers are permitted each day. 40m downstream of a hatchery – sign posted 'piscifactoría', there is a small pool where there are a large number of fish up to 2kg. The fish are very noticeable since the channel is only one metre wide at this point. To fish this pool, anglers often use a small Royal Coachman fly lure cast with a bubble float. The water level reduces a lot in the summer. Downstream of the dam wall, sign posted 'presa de embalse de Qentar' are caught mainly smaller brown trout. Barbel can be caught in the downstream stretch; they have swum up from the lower reservoir. Day tickets can be obtained locally from: Gran Vía de Colón, 48, Tel. 958276550. Description: 5km long, fish: upstream of Tocón downstream until the tail end of Quentar reservoir (a 2kg brown trout was recently caught from where the river enters the reservoir). Directions: from Granada head east on main road from Quéntar to La Peza. Access to some areas is good. The road runs parallel with the river, 15km to Granada.

2. **Coto de Alhama**, river Alhama, day ticket required, low mountain-water rules apply, Alhama de Granada (rainbow and brown trout) this river is a tributary of the river Genil. As with most rivers in Granada it's narrow with a lot of bank side cover. Artificial baits only. Ten bag limit. Fourteen anglers permitted per day, 8km long. Rainbow trout are an easy catch from a small reservoir sign posted 'pantaneta' using teaspoon spinning lures. By the end of the season they have grown to 1kg and if you're lucky from: 2kg-5kg. Brown trout, in addition to rainbows, are caught from the river but mainly along the upstream stretch away from the source of rainbow stocking in the small reservoir. On the upstream stretch there are a few small pools where anglers can attract smaller brown trout with a fly lure. Select a black emergent mayfly lure (baetis niger) at the start of the season then move onto a small sedge or a large brown mayfly lure by middle of May.

Description: 8km long. Start fishing upstream at the exit of the river Cerezal downstream to the tail end of the small reservoir, sign posted "pantaneta". Directions: Granada southwest A-338 to Alhama.   To access the upstream stretch go via Jatar then follow a track, this isn't signposted so ask in this way, "por fabor senor, donday ees el coto del río?" (please tell me the way to the river). This track runs all along the river bank and makes

THE SMOOTH GUIDE TO FLY FISHING IN SOUTHERN SPAIN AND THE COSTA RESORTS

for good access. The downstream stretch starts at a bar located by the small reservoir. This is a good place to enjoy lunch, 60km from Seville.

3. **Coto de Pantaneta**, day ticket required, low mountain-water rules apply, Alhama de Granada (rainbow trout). The small reservoir covers 5.4ha and fourteen anglers are permitted to fish here each day. There is a ten bag limit for rainbow trout The fishing reserve starts upstream at the gulley, sign posted "cortijo de la Zorrica" downstream until the dam wall.

4. **Coto de Quéntar**, embalse de Quéntar, day ticket required, low mountain-water fishing rules apply, Quéntar (rainbow trout). Baits authorised include spinning lures, sweetcorn and cooked potato. Ten bag limit for rainbow trout 40ha in area. Twenty five anglers are permitted to fish each day. Directions: Granada east to Quéntar, 15km.

5. **Coto de Fardes**, river Fardes, day ticket required, traditional fishing reserve rules apply, Huétor-Santillán (brown trout). Five bag limit. Eight anglers are permitted to fish each day. The fishing reserve is 11km long. This is one of the few rivers remaining that has preserved its original population of wild brown trout. Best to fish upstream of the old electric power station towards the small reservoir. Directions: A-92 northeast from Granada. Access to this stretch is via a dirt track for 2km-3km.

6. **Coto de Genazar**, river Genazar, day ticket required, traditional fishing reserve rules apply, Loja (rainbow trout) ten bag limit. Six anglers are permitted to fish each day. Reserve is 3.3km long. Previous complaints about poaching and dumping of dead fish near to the hatchery have stopped. Directions: Granada west A-329 to Loja.

7. **Coto de Riofrío**, river Riofrío / river Salado, Loja, day ticket required, (brown and rainbow trout) most sections are open all year, exceptions are stated below. Artificial baits only. Ten bag limit. Ten anglers are permitted to fish on working days; fifteen anglers are permitted at weekends and on public holidays.

Average channel width is 4m. The fishing reserve is managed by the Ayuntamiento (Loja town hall). The intensive fishing reserve is 4km long, fish from the source of the river Frío and a small hamlet on the river Salado, called Caserio de la Palanquilla, downstream until A-92 freeway bridge. The most popular swims are found in the last kilometre of the intensive fishing stretch.

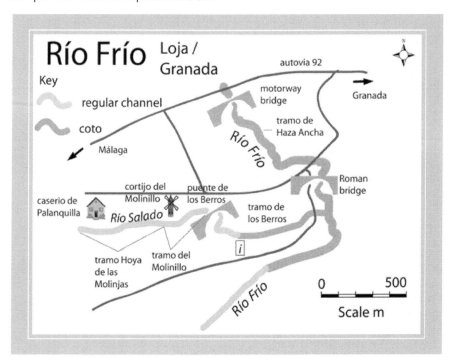

The river Frío section is as long as the river Salado but narrower, with an average channel width of just 2m-3m. The fishing reserve is open year round except on non-festive Mondays. Day tickets are available in advance from the environment agency office, located in Granada. From the motorway bridge, the river Frío is classed as a low mountain -water fishing reserve (sing posted 'coto de pesca baja montaña') open from the third Sunday in March until 15th August and the river stretch runs downstream for a further 3.2km ending by the A-92 freeway bridge.

The fishing reserve is located in the northeast foothills of the Sierra de Loja, one hour's drive west of Granada, where there exists one of the largest aquifer water reserves in Granada province. Recorded catches date back as far as 1664, but the river has become very popular with visitors over the last twenty years, with locals and foreigners alike. Trout live in pools with open river bank but also along stretches where the river passes through undergrowth and past galleries of poplar, willow and eucalyptus trees.

The last 800m of the downstream stretch, located by the confluence with the private fishing reserve is very suitable for nymph fishing at dusk especially by the bridge sign posted 'zona del Puente'. Other anglers prefer to fish in the clean waters of the upstream section, where there are three artificial pools. Larger fish are usually caught further downstream. Best to THE SMOOTH GUIDE TO FLY FISHING IN SOUTHERN SPAIN AND THE COSTA RESORTS use teaspoon lures - silver Mepps number two, at start of the day, fly lures from then on. Use a weighted nymph lure in the morning then, at midday in summer try a dry fly lure, for instance an emergent mayfly or a stonefly. In autumn midge fly types hook size twelve. Baitfish imitation lures, for instance streamers also work well here. This location offers a good atmosphere to fish in with lots of tourist spectators – a bit like the US Masters golf tournament; it's easy to catch rainbow trout approximately 1kg-2kg with the chance of some big ones, up to 5kg. Barbel and sturgeon have escaped from the nearby hatchery.

Fishing licence and day ticket: Alberge de Pescadores de Río Frío, Riviera de Riofrío s/n 18300 Loja (Granada) Tel, (0034) 958 32 31 77. Loja Town Hall Tel, 958 32 11 56. And from: Patronato Municipal de Turismo de Loja, C/Joaquín Costa s/n. 18300 Loja Tel & fax, 958 32 39 49. Directions: equidistant from Málaga and Granada (65km). A-92. The bailiff's number is more reliable when attempting to obtain day tickets, Tel, 605823933.

8. **Coto de Pinillos**, river Genil, day ticket required, intensive fishing reserve rules apply, Pinos Genil (brown and rainbow trout). Fishing is allowed all year. Ten bag limit. Artificial baits, only, 2.3km long. Ten anglers are permitted to fish on working days and fifteen anglers at weekends. A very effective fly lure is called imitación de hueva de salmon (imitation fish eggs). Banks become steep in places. Day tickets may be obtained from the town hall in Pinos Genil, sign posted 'ayuntamiento'. Tel, 958 48 87 72. Directions: 16km southeast from Granada.

10. **Coto de Cacín I**, river Cacín, day ticket required, low mountain-water fishing rules apply, catch and release, Cacín (brown trout). Artificial fly and spinner lures only: using a single barbless hook. Stretch is 4km long. Sixteen anglers are permitted to fish each day for both fishing reserves. Fish from the dam, sign posted 'presa de Bermejales' downstream until a Roman bridge. Directions: Granada southwest A-338 to presa de Bermejales. Access from: the old road that links Cazín with the dam is for the able bodied. And also from: the overflow of the dam. In addition, cross over the Roman Bridge and head upstream. The channel is surrounded by dense vegetation that can make access problematic, but far from impossible, and an angler is often rewarded with a catch.

10A. **Coto de Cacín II**, river Cacín, day ticket required, low mountain-water fishing rules apply, catch and release, Cacín (brown trout). Artificial fly and spinner lures only: use a single barbless hook. Stretch is 8km long, fish from the Roman Bridge until a bridge in Cacín and a dam wall called 'presa del Turro'. Gold Mepps number two spinning lures works well. Directions: Granada southwest A-338 to Cacin, GR-101 GR-180.

THE SMOOTH GUIDE TO FLY FISHING IN SOUTHERN SPAIN AND THE COSTA RESORTS

Fishermen have been visiting Riofrío since 1664

Day ticket stretch of the river Frío

Angel Cabrera, who runs Jaén fishing club, visits the intensive fishing reserve at the village of Riofrío located northwest of Granada, for a few days each year. He stays at nearby Hotel-Restaurante Paco Rama, situated next to the river, and he's able to purchase day tickets for catch and release fishing in his hotel bar from the local bailiff.
Angel's webpage address: http://csierrasur.net

"The bailiff usually turns up just after 8 a.m. and in return for presentation of passport will supply my day tickets for eighteen euros. There's always the possibility of bagging a half kilo rainbow trout, in the intensive fishing reserve, but many anglers believe it's less trouble to order a fish dish from the restaurant. Rainbow trout are stocked at regular intervals throughout the year and they are surprisingly robust fighters. There's an eight bag limit for rainbow trout whilst Andalusia law states that all wild brown trout must be returned safely to the water, irrespective of where they're caught.

In the middle of town, a peaceful fishing spot is found

THE SMOOTH GUIDE TO FLY FISHING IN SOUTHERN SPAIN AND THE
COSTA RESORTS

One point worth noting is that while other fisheries, found in Andalusia, are not at their best during the hot summer period, Riofrío is a consistent fish, year round. Even in the height of August, when Angel Cabrera visited, there is plenty of shade, afforded by trees found along the river bank. Fishing is best at dawn and dusk

Another attraction, for anglers, is the option of using a peculiar technique, which consists of employing a heavy ballasted nymph lure – a barbless hook, and using a spinning rod, a method similar to fly fishing but not exactly the same. It's not a method suitable for all rivers and lakes, and it requires short casts, in moderate current, in water deeper than one metre and an angler needs to keep hidden from trout. It also requires a level of skill similar to fly fishing and is considered well suited to Riofrío.

At weekends, many tourists visit attracted by chance to spot Riofrío's stocked trout and failing that, to visit fish farms and restaurants. Most family groups arrive from Granada, located 60km to the east. Anglers should avoid weekends and public holidays.

To be honest, this is not one of Granada's purest trout fisheries; the river is quite acceptable until it reaches the village, where the water becomes a little turbid. Under the A92 freeway bridge, by the containing dam that forms the downstream border of the fishing reserve, the water quality is questionable.

On my last visit, in August, the water level was low, considering that this river is quite shallow, and similar to the Penalta and El Duende. Nevertheless, as you can see from the photos, the river was very clear, quite clean in the downstream stretch, by the A92 freeway bridge and the containment dam. There were no bad smells, just a little stale air that's normal in summer along a halted river stretch.

Angel fishes by the Roman bridge

This has a lot to do with the significant presence of a water purification plant, operated by Loja council, who manage this fishing reserve with the bailiffs: they do a good job.

I began fishing next to the downstream boundary of the private fishing reserve, in a large pool by the Roman Bridge, which was no longer large because of the lack of water. I used a spinning rod with a nymph lure, judging bites by touch. The rest of this stretch is made up of smooth glides. The intensive fishing reserve extends for 3km through the village of Riofrío, average depth is 1.5m to 2m and it's only one metre wide in many places. Really just a stream and we kept to the same 800m wider stretch where the river Salado joins, which attracts other anglers. From the confluence of the Salado until the birth of the Riofrío is a privately owned, no-fishing stretch is sign posted 'vedado'.

A 3kg rainbow trout, caught by Angel from the upper part of the Riofrío

The majority of anglers employed nymph fishing techniques (submerged fly lures). The stretch shown in the photo is situated on the outskirts of Riofrío behind one of the many restaurants found here. And one of the disadvantages of fishing here is the noise caused by the proximity of the village. For this reason it's best to fish on working days.

In spite of the low volume, the water quality is very good in the downstream part, and much improved over previous years, the photos of docile fish in my arms do not do justice to the robust fight they put up.

Fishermen keep quiet, close to the river bank

The end of the fishing reserve, located below the A92 road bridge, until arriving at the containment raft has clean water, no rubbish. It's not as pretty as the rest of the reserve but acceptable all the same. At last the first catch of the day, after missing three bites – I required practice; I switched to casting a teaspoon spinning lure.

I cast into the current where it touches the retaining wall and forms an eddy in the middle of a small pool. There were many trout stationed here, feeding by rising and lowering in the current.

Casting a spinning lure rewarded me with one of the prettiest captures of the day, from this spot. Waders allow you to enter the river, but if you have none then get as close to the water's edge as possible. Let line out by reversing the reel handle.

Visitors can spot trout, but trout can always spot visitors first

Be careful to avoid a tangle. Keep a tense line, and keep the rod tip in the water to prevent the lure from surfacing. Let the power of the current work the action of the lure. The action of the lure must be kept at a slower pace than the speed of the current. Holding the lure up in the flow causes it to turn backwards like a crazy frog. And it's the action of the lure that entices fish to bite.

At 2pm I retired for lunch in Restaurante Paco Rama. The humidity, approaching midday, was something else and it was great to escape the afternoon, August heat. A cold beer went down well and so did another.

I resumed fishing at 6pm; the original intention was to fish 'zona del Salado', located north of the intensive fishing reserve. However the pool by the Roman Bridge proved more alluring. Late in the day the pool was crowded with rainbow trout and I caught three more by 6.45pm.

Irrespective of the method of fishing anglers decide to adopt or the type of fish species present, Riofrío is a special place that rarely fails to please, or reward with some fine catches and great memories. And because it has so many virtues it always keeps a few hidden from view. It's these secrets that visitors aim to discover and encourages anglers to return to Riofrío on many occasions."

Riofrio has just three hundred residents but fourteen restaurants, many serve local trout dishes. And a nearby sturgeon hatchery produces caviar that is exported to Russia.

Riofrío has more to offer than just fishing

Food connoisseurs should head to Riofrío where trout and caviar are the town's claim to fame. Riofrío is home to many trout hatcheries, which produce 500,000kg of fish annually and the world's first and only organic sturgeon farm. The purity of local spring water, used in production, contributes to producing the greatest caviar in all of Spain.

Piscifactoría de Sierra Nevada was founded, as a trout hatchery in 1964 in Riofrío, which is located high in the Sierra Nevada Mountains 60km west of Granada in southern Spain. The hatchery began to diversify into sturgeon in the late 1980s following a 90% decline in Beluga sturgeon, mainly in the Caspian Sea that used to provide the majority of Russian sourced caviar to the world.

A sturgeon is hatched, in captivity at Riofrío

Iberian sturgeon, Mediterranean identity

17 years later, and 29kg heavier a fish is stripped of its eggs

Fishing sturgeon for their meat and their edible eggs – caviar, was a common sight in Spain up until the early 1970s, from the coasts of the Mediterranean and the Atlantic to the Guadalquivir, Ebro, Duero and the Tajo Rivers. Adriatic (*A. naccarri*) and Atlantic (*A. sturio*) species, and even the occasional famous Beluga (*H.huso*) made an annual migration up Iberia's rivers in order to breed from their home in the surrounding seas and oceans.

The production of caviar from the river Guadalquivir used Atlantic sturgeon and between 1932 and 1970 five hundred fish were caught annually. The fish were processed at a factory called Fábrica de caviar de Coria del Río located near Seville until 1972 when it no longer caught enough fish to sustain its operation.

Historically caviar from the Iberian Peninsula was a famous desired delicacy. In fact, there existed a brand of Spanish caviar which was once exported by the tonne, every year with great success to countries such as Russia.

During these decades of production, over fishing of the Atlantic sturgeon, for its caviar, and the construction of the Alcalá del Río dam on the Guadalquivir near Seville meant that this species almost became extinct. Very few wild sturgeons have survived; the majority are Adriatic sturgeon, which remain in the river Po located in north east Italy.

▶**Caviar is an old Spanish delicacy**

Caviar was traditionally consumed as a way to add salt to cooking in Spain. Cervantes even mentions caviar in his great Spanish novel, Don Quixote in 1615.

"They stretched themselves on the ground, and making a tablecloth of the grass they spread upon it bread, salt, knives, walnut, scraps of cheese, and well-picked ham-bones which if they were past gnawing were not past sucking. They also put down a black dainty called, they say, caviar, made of the eggs of fish, a great thirst-awakener."

The factory, at Coria del Río during its heyday in the 1930's

Caviar production takes place at Riofrío today

Riofrío caviar sells at €60 for 30gms, half the price of wild, Beluga caviar

Andalusia may be famous for the caviar it used to process, from Atlantic sturgeon, but today the Riofrío hatchery breeds 98,000 Adriatic sturgeons annually. This species is smaller, growing up to 80kg and two metres long compared with 400kg and five metres for Atlantic sturgeon and it's endemic to the Mediterranean and Adriatic Seas– found nowhere else

The farm's production methods are unique in a number of ways. Most farms use hormones to make females mature faster (allowed to develop in their own time, female sturgeon can't be told apart from males until they are eight or nine years old and reach maturity some time between fifteen and twenty years). Riofrío hatchery is prepared to invest in time and good practice for the best results.

Then there is the quality of the water that feeds the pools in which the fish live, which is fed from a natural spring of the river Frío, it's filtered through reed beds and maintains a year-round temperature of thirteen to fifteen degrees.

A female Adriatic sturgeon typically weighs 30kg and is eighteen years old when she is considered ready for processing. Ten to fifteen per cent of whose body weight is judged to be eggs: a potential haul of up to 4.5kg. The timing is crucial. Harvest too early and the eggs may be dry because they haven't yet absorbed fat from the fish's belly; too late and they may lack definition and structure.

Nothing goes to waste; after the eggs are extracted the sturgeon's thick, grey-black skin goes to Italy where it's used in handbag manufacture."

For further information contact: Piscifactoría de Sierra Nevada, S.L. Camino de la Piscifactoría, 2. 18313 Riofrío (Granada) Tel, 958 322 621, Fax: 958 321 114. www.caviarperse.net

A sturgeon is hauled from the river Guadalquiver, near Seville during the 1940's

After fishing, enjoy your evening meal

Riofrío's most popular dish is trout steamed in tomato, garlic, and onions. For dinner you might try some trout, pan-fried in a little bit of olive oil and fresh garlic. A great wine that will complement any fish dish, this bottle of red comes from Córdoba.

Restaurants are plentiful in Riofrío - Mesón Alazor, Rama Palacios, Paco Rama, Restaurante Fernández, Restaurante Los Jiménez and Mesón Rio Frío offer quiet spots to enjoy a cold beer or tasty glass of cold sherry - with tapas followed by a stunning meal.

▶ **Caviar recipe - Mezzalunas**

These tapas are easy to prepare and look like ravioli but with thin slices of potato in place of pasta, half of them stuffed with smoked *petits pois* (small French peas) individually peeled so that it is almost the same size as a sturgeon's egg and the rest filled with caviar that has been warmed but not cooked, over which are scattered a few raw blanched almonds and gossamer threads of orange zest.

River Castil

11. Coto de Castril, river Castril, day ticket required, catch and release, high mountain-water fishing rules apply, Castril de las Peñas (wild brown trout). Wonderful setting: found within Sierra Nevada National Park.

Fishing is permitted from the first Sunday in June until 30th September. It's a tributary of the river Guadiana Menor. This is a great river to fish for wild brown trout that feed on the abundant insect life specifically sedges, mayfly and stonefly. The river has never been stocked.

Description: fish from Barranco de la Magdalena downstream until puente de Lézar. Twelve anglers are permitted each day, along a 5km stretch. A forest track provides good access, parallel to the channel. Day tickets: Bar la Cochera in Castril. Otherwise consult with the environment agency office in Granada.

Recommended fly lures include hare's ear nymph in olive and natural colours, size twelve hooks. Large mayfly imitation dry fly lures in light brown and olive, size sixteen and eighteen hook. Parachute fly lures, in same colour as mayfly lures, size sixteen and eighteen hook. Red deer hair sedge fly lures, in several sizes and shape, size sixteen and eighteen hook. It's always advisable to carry larger sedge fly lures, size twelve hooks, which imitate large stoneflies that inhabit this river.

Seca pardón is an indispensable large, brown, dry fly lure for use in spring, in mature rivers and at start of summer in mountain streams. Use it when you observe unmistakable hatchings of mayfly at noon.

Directions: reserve is accessed easily along a path 3km from Fatima for 2km before Castril. If you follow the signs for the campsite you won't be too far off. Granada northeast A-92 at Gaudix take A-92N exit north at La Venta A-315 to Castril. 3km from Fatima: 2km before Castril. Follow road signs for the campsite. Access is easy.

THE SMOOTH GUIDE TO FLY FISHING IN SOUTHERN SPAIN AND THE COSTA RESORTS

Fishing the river Castril in summer

Alex fishes a long glide

In June 2009 Rafa Muñoz and his fishing buddy Alex promised themselves a short fishing break, somewhere not too remote but peaceful and beautiful.

After approximately ninety minutes drive, north east from Granada, they arrived at Castril Natural Park. Here they spent a couple of days fishing the intensive reserve of the river Castril located near Baza.

"The Castril is very different from the rivers of the Sierra Nevada, it has cloudy water. In spite of its turbid nature it's perfect for fly fishing.

Castril Natural Park is a wonderful location. Vultures were spotted, flying overhead, using thermals created by the mountains to rise gracefully above the midday heat.

Rafa casts a nymph lure into the current, using a large boulder for cover

A beautiful brown trout, caught by Alex from the river Castril

THE SMOOTH GUIDE TO FLY FISHING IN SOUTHERN SPAIN AND THE
COSTA RESORTS

Spotting a fish, Alex wades upstream to investigate

The heat at midday was unbearable and the trout had taken a siesta. One good point, this is the period for spawning and we spotted many juvenile trout and this bodes well for the future of fishing on the river Castril."

Our accommodation, Camping El Cortijillo

San Clement reservoir

13. **Coto de embalse San Clemente**, San Clemente reservoir, day ticket required, upland water rules apply, Huéscar (brown and rainbow trout) 168ha in area, twenty anglers are permitted to fish each day. Baits allowed: artificial fly and spinning lures plus sweetcorn, beans and *masilla* (paste type hook bait) ten bag limit for rainbow trout. Handy access: straight to the shoreline. Quiet place to fish and relax, clear water means that you must be careful to avoid scaring the fish. Many carp to 2kg are caught using fly lures and some trout are present. Especially worth a cast from where the Guardal and Raigadas Rivers enter the tail end of the reservoir, upstream a little, until their confluence. Directions: Granada northeast A-92 then A-92N exit north at Cúllar Baza A-330 to Huéscar now west A-326 Puente Duda on a local road: heading north towards the dam wall, sign posted "presa".

Embalse de Canales is classed as an official trout fishing water. It's catch and release reservoir, a day ticket is required and upland water rules apply. Coarse fishing is permitted here all year. Anglers sometimes need to descend steep rocky slopes in order to access some parts of the shoreline where large trout, exceeding 5kg have been caught recently using large Norwegian baitfish fly lures. Take care!

River Genil by the aqueduct bridge

12. **Coto de Genil**, river Genil, day ticket required, high mountain-water fishing rules apply, catch and release, Güéjar-Sierra (brown trout). The river Genil flows through the city of Granada but the best fishing is found further upstream towards the mountains of the Sierra Nevada. River channel is contained by a series of terraced, steep inclines in many places. A few small pools: and runs. Riverbed is covered with stones of varying size. Casting is limited to 4m or 5m. Spot fish in lee of rocks in the current. Average channel width is 5m-8m.

Fly fishing only with a single barbless hook is allowed. Ten anglers are permitted each day. Stretch is 5.4km long. Fish from downstream: between the power station, sign posted 'central eléctrica' (situated 950m above sea level) but located downstream of Güejar Sierra. Make your way upstream to the confluence with the river San Juan (situated 1,175m above sea level). This is a good looking reserve; the local restaurants serve tasty trout dishes. Directions: located 16km southeast from Granada by the foothills of the Sierra Nevada. Upon arriving in Güéjar-Sierra, take the turn for Maitena: now there is an option. Head down: towards the power station for the downstream section of the fishing reserve. Park up by the power station and fish upstream. Or: continue towards Maitena to fish the upstream section. There are more access points this way, where the road runs parallel to the channel.

THE SMOOTH GUIDE TO FLY FISHING IN SOUTHERN SPAIN AND THE COSTA RESORTS

Rafa wades upstream, on Genil fishing reserve

THE SMOOTH GUIDE TO FLY FISHING IN SOUTHERN SPAIN AND THE
COSTA RESORTS

14. **Coto de Treveléz**, river Treveléz, high mountain-water fishing rules apply, day ticket required, Treveléz (pronounced tre-be-leth) and Busquístar (brown trout and a few rainbow trout) the river Trevélez is situated on the southern slopes of the Sierra Nevada, 1,650m above sea level, in the Alpujarras region, where the slopes are much more gently inclined than rivers located on the north facing aspect - and where the current is faster and stronger. Access points are good, and the river banks are pretty even.

Five bag limit. Ten anglers are permitted each day. Description: Stretch is 9.8km long, fish from: upstream at the boundary of the Sierra Nevada National Park downstream until the drainage channel called 'Acequia de Busquístar, found close to the bridge at Trévelez. Avoid public holidays when heavy traffic on narrow switchback mountain roads will slow your progress. The river Treveléz, Spain's highest village and the fishing reserve is easy to find using a road map.

Best to visit in June and early July before the water level drops. Many fish are caught in the downstream section of the river Trevélez despite its litter problem. Free fishing stretches begin in town and continue downstream and these sections contains lots of good fish. Directions: 80km southeast from Granada N-323, exit east, A348 at Beznar (the dam wall has a great view), then take local roads to Trévelez – a campsite is found here.

15. **Coto de embalse del Portillo**, high mountain-water fishing rules, day ticket required, catch and release, Castril (brown trout) the reservoir is fed by the river Castril (a free fishing section begins below the dam wall). The reservoir covers 74 ha, ten anglers are permitted to fish each day. Fishing is permitted from Lezar Bridge until the dam wall. Only fly fishing is allowed.

Embalse del Portillo

THE SMOOTH GUIDE TO FLY FISHING IN SOUTHERN SPAIN AND THE COSTA RESORTS

Treveléz fishing reserve, below Spain's highest village

Follow the sign, for Treveléz fishing reserve, 90 minutes drive south east from the city of Granada. Make an early start to avoid delays, or stay overnight in the local villages, to ensure you're up to fishing at dawn.

THE SMOOTH GUIDE TO FLY FISHING IN SOUTHERN SPAIN AND THE COSTA RESORTS

Mentioned below are free fishing stretches where upland water rules apply (*aguas de alta montaña* - a shorter fishing season occurs here) these fisheries support brown trout populations.

Genil River basin

River Dílar, Dílar (brown trout). The fishing reserve is 9km long. Fifteen anglers are permitted to fish each day. The river's source is located within the Sierra Nevada National Park (where you can't fish). But the fishing reserve lies just outside and has lost the fierce torrent characteristic of Andalusia's mountain rivers. Even so there's fast current that passes through a series of short runs on a very clear river bottom of stones and sand, which is the exception for riverbeds located in the Sierra Nevada.

Very clear water that requires above average fishing techniques. Fish the upstream stretch. Downstream of the town there is little current, and between here and the power station irrigation schemes extract much water, in summer the channel is dry. Fish from the boundary of the sign posted boundary of the Sierra Nevada National Park: towards Dilar. Directions: 15km south from Granada N-323 to Dílar - a campsite is found here: through town then 2km further on to the river located by the power station. Access track runs parallel to the channel.

River Genil: fish from the downstream boundary of Pinilos fishing reserve located by 'contra-embalse de Canales': towards Punete Verde de Granada, fly fishing only.

River Maitena, free fishing, Güéjar-Sierra (brown trout) the fishing reserve is 16km long. Twenty anglers are permitted to fish each day. Maitena is an Arabic word; it translates as 'the beautiful thing' and the setting lives up to expectations. It's possible to fish from the confluence with the river Genil until the boundary with the Sierra Nevada National Park. The river Maitena is best suited to spinning because the dense vegetation causes problems when casting a fly lure. Water level goes low in summer. Directions: 18km southeast from Granada. The river Mateina is found 2km further on from Güéjar-Sierra.

Embalse de Canales: fish from the power station sign posted 'central de Guejar-Sierra' towards the dam wall.

River Monachil: fish from the boundary of Sierra Nevada National Park in a downstream direction.

Guadiana Menor River basin

River Alhama: Lugros, fish from the boundary of Sierra Nevada National Park in a downstream direction.
River Bravatas: fish from the stream's source towards a ravine called cortijo del Doctor.
River Castril: fish from the dam wall, sign posted 'Presa del Portillo' in a downstream direction.

River Guardal: fish from the dam wall of embalse de San Clemente towards a bridge crossing the A-326 road and from a hatchery, sign posted 'piscifactori' towards the confluence with the Raigaidas stream, fly fishing only.

Zonas Del Marquesado, Jares, Lanteira, Aldeire, Dólar and Hueneja, fish downstream from the sing posted boundary of Sierra Nevada National Park.

Guadalfeo River basin (the Alpujarras region is 1 ½ hour's drive south east from Granada on a combination of freeway and good mountain roads).

Chico, Dúrcal, Guadalfeo, Lanjarón, Mecina, Nechite, Torrente, Trevélez, Poqueira and Valor Rivers can be fished downstream from the boundary with Sierra Nevada National Park.

River Poqueira: fish downstream from Poqueira hydro-electric power-station. At this point it's classed as catch and release, upland fishery (sign posted 'pesca sin muerte: aguas de alta montaña) and is 1,750m above sea level (approximately 5,500 feet).

The abandoned village of Poqueira sits at an altitude approximately 1500m / 4500 feet above sea level. The two penultimate villages offer places to spend time relaxing and eating. Great views of Pico de Tajo (3,088m above sea level) can be enjoyed as your vehicle winds its way along switch back roads, climbing towards Poqueira power station (at Sierra Nevada National Park boundary, refer to picture shown on page 124). Nearby villages provide restaurants and accommodation; the views across the mountains, down to the sea from Bubión and Pampaneira are outstanding.

The following fisheries are free fishing stretches that do not contain brown trout, as a rule but do contain rainbow trout.
River Padules: fish along its whole length
River Riofrío: fish from Rute road-bridge towards the confluence with the river Genil

Almeria

Almería province is one of the sunniest and driest places in Spain. The desert terrain limits fishing opportunities, but you can still find good swims to cast your line.

Fishing licence and day tickets: C/Hermanos Machado 4, 4a Planta 04004 Almeria Tel, 950 01 11 40

Further information: Delegación Provincial de Medio Ambiente Reyes Católicos, 43 04071. Almería. Tel, 950 01 28 00

20. **Coto de Andarax**, river Andarax, day ticket required, catch and release, high mountain–water fishing rules apply, Laujar de Andarax (brown trout). Open from the second Sunday in May until 30th September. Use single barbless hooks, only flyfishing and spinning lures are allowed. Requires a good walk from town uphill to the fishing area, which is well signposted. The reserve is 5.9km long, and a maximum of four anglers are permitted to fish each day from the junction of Barranco del Aguadero downstream until a recreation facility sign posted 'Badén de la Adecuación recreativa', there is a sealed ford, recreational area called 'El Nacimiento'. Day tickets may be purchased from the water bailiff (agente forestal) by the river bank. Directions: from Almería head northwest N-340 A348 to Laujar de Andarax.

Free fishing for trout is allowed on the following upland streams

River Ohanes (Andarax River basin): fish from boundary of Sierra Nevada National Park until a road bridge connecting Ohanes with Beires.

River Paterna (Adra river Basin): fish from boundary of Sierra Nevada National Park towards a road bridge connecting Laujar with Paterna.

River Bayárcal (Adra river Basin): fish from boundary of Sierra Nevada National Park towards a road bridge connecting Bayárcal with Laroles. Free fishing is allowed in the following rivers that do not contain brown trout but do contain rainbow trout

River Nacimiento and tributaries, and river Ohanes: fish from boundary of Sierra Nevada National Park.

THE SMOOTH GUIDE TO FLY FISHING IN SOUTHERN SPAIN AND THE COSTA RESORTS

River Andarax in flood

No fishing areas (sign posted 'Refugios de pesca'): include the river Andarax from the boundary of Sierra Nevada National Park park towards the junction with barranco del Aguadero, and this is where the fishing reserve begins.

If you happen to experience difficulty obtaining an Andalusia freshwater fishing licence, John Wrenn of Mojacár Angling Club in Almeria may be able to help out for a small charge. Contact details:

Beachcomber Bar/Restaurant (Underneath Crown Rentacar) on Mojacár Playa, Almeria, Spain.Contact John Wrenn Tel, 0034 950 473 099. E-mail address: beachcomberjohn@gmail.com

Letters to The Beachcomber Bar/Restaurant: Box 33 Ave Andalucía 22 edif Multicentro, local 25, 04638, Mojacár, Almeria, Spain.

Cádiz

Cádiz province contains the town of Jerez, famous for its Sherry vineyards. Sierra de Grazalema Natural Park is found north of Seville, it supports some promising wild brown trout fisheries. Observant visitors may notice a sign 'Granado Suelto' as they venture across an open field, in order to access a river. The sign's literal translation means "seeded loose", the land is owned by livestock breeders and the animals in question are called el 'torro bravo' (fighting bulls).

Fishing licence and day tickets: Delegación Provincial de Medio Ambiente: Plaza Asdrúbal, s/n. Edeficio Junta de Andalucía, 3 planta 11071 Cádiz. Tel, 956 00 87 00 Fax, 956 00 87 02 & 956 00 87 03. E-mail address: Delegada.ca.cma@juntadeandalucia.es

Cádiz trout fisheries

1. **Coto de El Bosque**, river Mojaceite, day ticket required, low mountain-water fishing rules apply, El Bosque (brown and rainbow trout) open from first Sunday in March until 31st August. Artificial baits only. Ten bag limit for rainbow trout. The reserve is 10km long and ten anglers are permitted to fish each day from, the source of the Benamahoma stream downstream until overflow channel, sign posted 'desagüe del arroyo de la Almaja'. Directions: A-376 from Marbella to Ronda then A-372 to El Bosque.Free day tickets are required from El Bosque park office: Oficina Parque Natural Sa de Grazalema, Avda. Diputacíon, s/n. Tel, 956 71 60 63 / 62 36.

El Bosque fishing reserve, located on the river Mojaceite

Located in northeast Cádiz province, Sierra de Grazalema Natural Park contains the famous white-mountain villages, for example Zahara. The hills and valleys are beautifully green and they are home to one hundred pairs of Griffen Vultures nesting in the Gargunta and Seca gorges.

Sierra de Grazalema Natural Park is famous for its trout fishing and hill walking, spring and autumn are the best times to visit. And Europe's southernmost trout stream is located at El Bosque. Day tickets can be booked in advance, and collected at Zahara if preferred.

No fishing areas (sign posted 'vedados de pesca') include all the *lagunas* (natural lakes) found in Cádiz province and the following streams, arroyos del Saladillo, Saguzal, Garzos, Mojón Blanco, Santiago, Salado de Espera, Val de Hondo and Salado de Morón from their source until the border with the province of Seville. Full details are given in the free booklet called 'Pesca Continental en Andalucía' issued annually by the environment agency offices in major towns and cities.

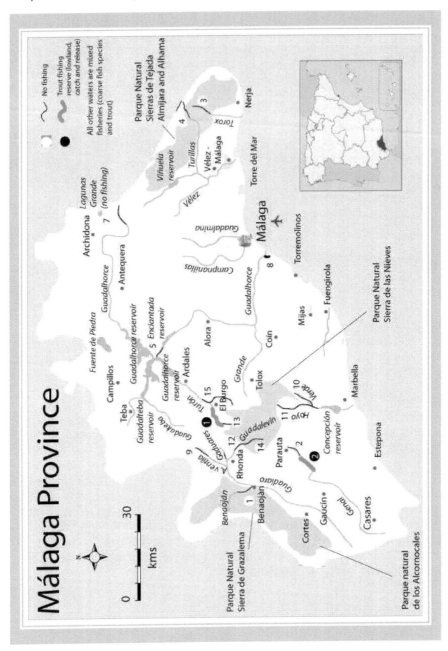

THE SMOOTH GUIDE TO FLY FISHING IN SOUTHERN SPAIN AND THE COSTA RESORTS

Málaga

Málaga's main industry and claim to fame is its tourist resorts, particularly those on the beaches along the Costa del Sol (Sun Coast). These beaches are visited by millions of European tourists. But besides the beaches, the mountainous province has some good fishing rivers and an American Black bass lake called embalse de la Concepción is located near Marbella.

Fishing licence and day tickets: Delegación Provincial de Medio Ambiente: c/ Mauricio Moro Paseto, 2. Edificio Eurocom, Bloque sur, planta 3 y 4. 29071. Málaga. Tel, 951 04 00 58, fax, 951 04 01 08. E-mail address: Delegado.ma.cma@juntadeandalucia.es

UK angler Richard Hewitt tackles a barbel near Málaga

THE SMOOTH GUIDE TO FLY FISHING IN SOUTHERN SPAIN AND THE COSTA RESORTS

Málaga's trout and barbel fisheries

1. **Coto de Cabecera del Turón**, river Turón, day ticket required, low mountain-water fishing rules apply, catch and release, El Burgo (brown trout). Fly fishing or spinning lure only allowed: with a single barbless hook. Four bag limit. Minimum size is 22cm. Reserve is 6km long. Five anglers are permitted to fish each day from the irrigation channel dam, called presa de acequia, located between the first and second dykes downstream until a road bridge connecting El Burgo with Casarabonela. Directions: Ronda east A-366 to El Burgo.

2. **Coto de Genal**, river Genal, day ticket required, low mountain-water fishing rules apply, catch and release, Igualeja, Pujerra, Juzcar and Farajan (brown trout). Fly fishing and spinner lures only allowed. Reserve is 5.5km in long. Five anglers are permitted to fish each day from the confluence with the river Seco downstream until Farajan municipal boundary. The water is very clean. Directions: Marbella west A-7 then north A-376 in direction of Ronda. Exit west on local roads to Igualeja.

Embalse de la Concepción, Istan (Black bass). Fish from the bank: at the dam. Or hire a boat (guide service offered) at the Istan country Club situated by the reservoir. From a boat use # 6 line. A good alternative to imitation bait fly lures like poppers are deer hair and mouse imitations, these have a similar effect. When the fly lure gets wet and heavy you may find it easier to cast with a #7 or # 8 line. Especially with wet fly lures, when a faster retrieve gets action going. Purists will stick with surface lures. This venue is not generally recognised as a trout-water but there may be some fish present. All types of bait may be employed. Directions: Marbella west A-7/E-15 5 km then exit north local road towards Istan.

La Toba fishing reserve, on the river Segura

THE SMOOTH GUIDE TO FLY FISHING IN SOUTHERN SPAIN AND THE
COSTA RESORTS

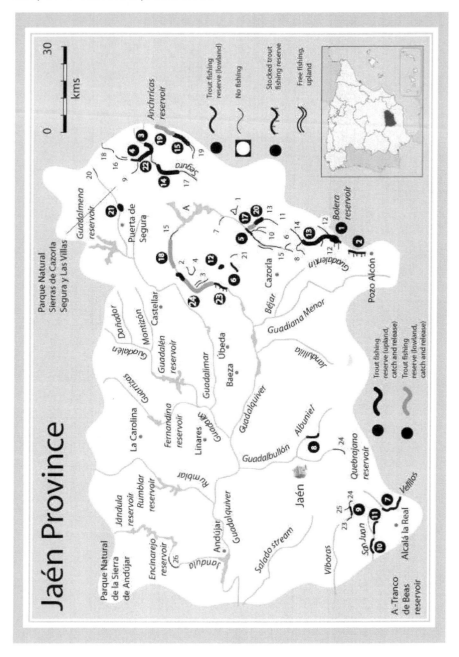

THE SMOOTH GUIDE TO FLY FISHING IN SOUTHERN SPAIN AND THE
COSTA RESORTS

Jaén

Although it is one of the least known provinces of Spain, Jaén has many wonderful rivers and many brown trout fisheries begin their journey in Sierra de Cazorla, Segura and Las Villas Natural Parks. Anglers not only enjoy excellent game fishing but experience magnificent scenery. The natural parks' cold, mountain-rivers are best visited from June onwards in order to allow time for the water to warm up and the trout to feed.

Leisure activities for Cazorla Natural Park include kayaking and canoeing, hiking, photography, horse riding, mountain biking, botanical gardens, bird watching.

Plenty of day tickets are left over from the pre-season annual draw, they're made available during the fishing season through local bars and restaurants. The parks office in Cazorla, their address is given below and the environment agency office in Jaén can also help.

A numbers placed before fisheries mentioned below denote angling locations shown on the Jaén provincial map shown above.

Fishing licence and day tickets: Delegación Provincial de Medio Ambiente: Fuente Del Serbo, 3. 23071 Jaén Tel, 953 01 24 00

Day tickets are also available from: Oficina Del Parque de Cazorla, C/Martínez Falero, 11 Tel, 953 720102, fishing reserves – 953720125.

Unless stated otherwise fly and spinning lures, sweetcorn and *masilla* (fishmeal ground bait) is allowed.

Jaén's trout fisheries

Bolera reservoir provides good trout fishing opportunities

1. **Embalse de la Bolera**, river Guadalentín, day ticket required, low mountain-water fishing rules apply, Pozo Alcón and Peal de Becerro, (rainbow trout, barbel and carp). The reservoir covers 258ha. Fishing is permitted from the third Sunday in March until 30th November, for sixty anglers each day. Day tickets are available from the town hall, sign-posted 'Ayuntamiento de Pozo Alcón', Tel, 953 73 80 41 and from the park's office, Oficina Del Parque de Cazorla, C/Martínez Falero, 11 Tel, 953 72 01 02. Anglers may also like to try for day tickets at the park's office, Casa Forestal La Bolera, found on road connecting Pozo Alcón to Huéscar, ilometer road marker ten.

Crystal clear water surrounded by superb mountain backdrop of the Sierra Cazorla Natural Park. The water temperature remains cool even in August and the trout are sometimes hard to find but there are barbel and carp including royals that can also be caught using a fly lure. A campsite exists at the southern tip of the reservoir and Pozo Alcón is a tourist town with a good choice of accommodation and restaurants.

5. **Coto Puente Del Hacha**, river Guadalquivir (pronounced gua-dull-key-beer), day ticket required, high mountain-water fishing rules apply, Santiago-Pontones, La Iruela and Santo Tomé (rainbow trout) ten anglers are permitted to fish during the week and fifteen anglers at weekends and on public holidays. Fish along a 5km reach from Hacha Bridge downstream until the confluence with the river Borosa. Local anglers employ a weighted hare's ear nymph lure with success. Day tickets are available from. the park's office, Oficina Del Parque de Cazorla Tel, 953 72 01 02.

River Guadalquiver

7. **Coto Velillos**, river Frailes, day ticket required, low mountain-water fishing rules apply, Frailes and Alcalá la Real, (rainbow trout) ten anglers are permitted each day to fish from Cueva Bridge downstream until the confluence with the river Mures. A local angling club called Asociación de Pesca Deportiva El Chorrillo de Frailes is very helpful. Their president is called Francisco Medina Pareja. His members catch trout up to 2kg. Day tickets are available from the town hall, Ayuntamiento de Frailes Tel, 953 59 30 02. Directions: located on border: between provinces of Granada and Jaén. From Granada northwest N-432 to Alcalá then: JV-2262 northeast to Frailes.

COTO DE
PESCA
INTENSIVO

TRAMO
PARA LA PRACTICA
DE PESCA SIN MUERTE
(Con mosca artificial)

Trout catch from....   .....Hondo, catch and release fishery

12. **Coto Aguadero Hondo**, river Aguadero, day ticket required, low mountain-water fishing rules apply, Villacarrillo (rainbow trout) fifteen anglers are permitted to fish during the week and twenty anglers at weekends and on public holidays. Fishing takes place in a reservoir covering 26.4ha from the third Sunday in March until 12th October. Day tickets are available from the park's office, Oficina Del Parque de Cazorla Tel, 953 72 01 02. Anglers may also try for day tickets at the park's office, Casa Forestal de la Fresnedilla located by the reservoir.

This is a place of exceptional beauty and the quality of the fishing is reflected in the exceptional surroundings. Larger specimens are caught by the dam wall where most catches exceed 26cm in length and many exceed 32cm.

15. **Coto de Cortjo del Vado**, river Zumeta, day ticket required, low mountain-water fishing n rules apply, catch and release, Santiago-Pontones (brown trout), 5.7km stretch from a dam sign posted "presa de Palomares" until a ford called cortijo del Vado. Day tickets are available from the town hall, sign posted 'Ayuntamiento' de Santiago Pontones Tel, 953 43 80 02 and from Oficina Del Parque de Cazorla Tel, 953 72 01 02.

THE SMOOTH GUIDE TO FLY FISHING IN SOUTHERN SPAIN AND THE COSTA RESORTS

Fly fishing on the river Guadalquiver over three seasons

A view from Rafa's home - as he leaves, at dawn for a day's fishing. The summits of the Sieera Nevada are covered in snow in spring.

Rafael Muñoz is an expert fly fisherman and his backyard, Andalusia, contains trout fishing rivers found in the foothill's of Granada's Sierra Nevada and Jaén's Sierra Cazorla National Parks, these fisheries are worthy of any angler's attention. Here, Rafa gives a first hand account of fishing, for wild brown trout, at one of his favourite destinations a fishing reserve called 'coto Puente Ortega' found on the river Guadalquiver.

Rafa's excellent fishing blog contains invaluable information, and excellent advice about fishing rivers found in Granada and Jaén provinces. http://rafamcriado.blogspot.com
To get in touch with Rafa, email: supertochoarmilla@yahoo.es

►**The end of spring**

"Many anglers experience blank sessions when fishing the river Guadalquiver but on its day, this exciting location can provide a rewarding experience.

Córdoban and friend, Paco Carmona

We left before dawn, in the Sierra Nevada – our home, in order to reach Jaén for the first day of the fishing season. There blew a refreshing, morning breeze and the start of the day felt promising.

The river level was up. And, to my taste, there was too much wind, the water was slightly cloudy, too much noise came from the village, and I noticed fluctuations in current caused by releases from a reservoir called 'embalse del Tranco'. Fluctuations in water level are quite common and anglers should be made aware of the potential threat caused by such events. Everything foretold that an uninspiring day's fishing lay ahead.

My angling buddy, for the day, was Carmona Alpaca and you can see Paco, shown in the photo above, casting a nymph lure into the swirling current. The water temperature was fresh and there were no insect hatches all day. It's the end of spring and it's not warm enough for conditions required by insects to hatch.

A brown trout, caught using a parachute lure in the Sierra Nevada

Coto Puente Ortega supports beautiful trout but they're wary of anglers. To hold a fish, in our hands, is like taking extreme care with a papyrus document from the ancient library at Alexandria in Egypt.

At noon, we met at the Venta del Pino, to enjoy lunch and to compare our morning catches

The day started with just a few bites but without doubt things would improve. To capture the sights and sounds, of the Guadalquiver valley, is the greatest prize for a fisherman.

The wind grew stronger, but luckily the current remained constant. Conditions did not encourage dry fly fishing tactics and in spite of my enthusiasm, for this fishing method, I achieved little success. Instead I decided to use a weighted hare's ear nymph and suddenly my luck changed, I caught a fish. The photo below shows my first catch."

▶**We returned in May**

"Plenty of fish were visible, now that the water had warmed, but they proved elusive to the fly lure. Sight casting was the order of the day, we had to concentrate very hard, keep quiet and persevere. The trout were fussy; any errors in presentation, inaccurate casting or noise would spook the fish. After trying numerous, different fly lures I cast a dark olive mayfly fly lure into a glide and bingo! The water's surface breaks and indicates that a great days' fishing lies ahead.

Rafa's brown trout catch

The mayfly lure really hit the spot and many trout were rising, to it, well into the afternoon. As dusk settled activity in the pools increased. A brace of trout were feeding to within a couple of metres of my feet. As I left the river bank I wished the day had never ended. Retiring to dinner, I was mentally exhausted and took an early bed. "

My fishing buddies, at Venta del Pino: from the right Rafa Partera, myself, Paco Carmona and Rafael de Juan

▶The river Guadalquiver is "magic" in June

This wasn't the last time I was to experience hot conditions, but on this occasion the ambience of the mountains and the river gave me a positive attitude towards the days' fishing.

"There are places, found along the river Qualdalquiver, which really demonstrates how insignificant the angler really is. Pools where the trout have a healthy advantage over the angler and your fishing skills must attain a high level of expertise, in order to succeed in deceiving a fish.

Clear water means it's not an easy place to fish, but that's the great challenge, for the angler who's a fan of this fishing reserve. To improve, technically, until one day's fishing surpasses everything that went before and achieve success, but even then the quality of life that the valley offers is the real prize on offer.

A memorable day, spent fly fishing for wild brown trout

It seemed that the trout were more interested in celebrations, occurring in town, than they were in our fly lures. In spite of our best efforts, accurately casting to all corners of the river, pools, shady areas, riffles and glides, nothing was happening. The height, of the surrounding summits couldn't prevent the wind that was rocking the pine trees obstructing our view of the fish.

We fished two stretches of the river Guadalquiver and experienced the same bad luck. On Tuesday we fished the upstream stretch, located up to the fishing reserve's boundary signpost. On Wednesday we fished the downstream stretch, from the ford, which starts among olive groves. The downstream stretch gave me a better feeling, made memorable by a specimen catch.

A promising fishing pool

Rafa patiently casts a nymph lure into a pool

THE SMOOTH GUIDE TO FLY FISHING IN SOUTHERN SPAIN AND THE
COSTA RESORTS

Casting a lure

Now you can understand the spell that's cast by the river Gualdalquiver. The water kisses the stones and slips by our waders. We attempt to spot fish on the surface, checking for any disturbance in the current, and deciding, in the blink of an eye, whether to strike or not.

In the end, every angler has to call a halt to the day and retire for dinner. Before leaving, we glanced back at the wonderful river view and embraced the place like a faithful friend and said goodbye until next time. "

Rafa and his friends enjoyed lunch at Venta del Pino, kilometre road marker 10, Ctra. Tranco, Tel, 953128239. Visitors can book a room for the night at Hotel Losan. Ctra Tranco s / n. Cañada Morales Hornos de Segura. Jaén, Spain, Tel, 953495088.

17. **Coto Borosa**, river Borosa, day ticket required, low mountain-water fishing rules apply, catch and release, Santiago-Pontones and la Irueal (brown trout), 3.4km stretch from Charco Pancica Bridge downstream until the confluence with Truchas stream. Day tickets are available from the park's office, Oficina Del Parque de Cazorla Tel, 953 72 01 02. Anglers may also try enquiring after day tickets at the hatchery sign posted 'piscifactoría del río Borosa'. Pretty brown trout are small but plucky. Anglers who fish here also recommend the catch and release fishing reserve located near to Camping del Puente de Herrerias found along the river Guadalquiver. The downstream stretch is less noisy.

18. **Coto Puente Ortega**, river Guadalquiver, day ticket required, low mountain-water fishing rules apply, catch and release Villanueva Del Arzobispo and Sorihuela Del Guadalimar (brown trout, barbel and shad). Ten anglers are permitted to fish each day along a 9.6km stretch from 300m downstream of Los Agustines Bridge downstream until Peñon Del Caballo. Fly and spinner lures using a single barbless hook only.

Sedge and mayfly imitation fly lures work well. From the border with a stream called arroyo Chillar fly fishing only is allowed, downstream of this point spinner lures are permitted, both fishing techniques require a single barbless hook. Day tickets are available from the park's office, Oficina Del Parque de Cazorla Tel, 953 72 01 02. Rafael Munoz's account of fly fishing at Puente Ortega starts here.

19. **Coto Tramo Tobos**, river Zumeta, day ticket required, low mountain rules apply, catch and release, Santiago-Pontones (brown trout) ten anglers are permitted to fish along a 8.6km stretch from a ford called 'cortijo de Vado' downstream to where the river enters Vieja reservoir. Fly and spinner lures with a single barbless hook only. Day tickets are available from the town hall, sign posted 'Ayuntamiento' de Santiago Pontones, Tel, 953 43 80 02 and from the park's office, Oficina Del Parque de Cazorla Tel, 953 72 01 02. Best fished: with a dry fly lure or nymph. The trout are quite small but there are plenty of them about and they are caught up to 32cm though more frequently up to 23cm.

►**Autumn affords us one last chance**

River Guadalquiver has the Sierra Cazorla for a backdrop

October 2010, is the penultimate day of the fishing season. Another fishing season has passed but there's still time for one last visit to Puente Ortega fishing reserve. The options to fish other reserves are limited but the fishing season, for catch and release reserves found in Jaén, extends into October and this applies to our location.

"I left mid-morning. I obtained permits for two day' fishing and upon arrival crystalline waters, found in so much of the reserve's glides, gave a good omen for a successful fishing trip. The temperature is perfect; the surroundings emit a calm effect on visitors. Deciduous trees retain their leaves and the pines are always present.

Casting towards the rip line

One of the entrances to the fishing reserve is marked by a wild fig tree, surrounded by brambles, and there are more brambles found by the river bank. A path, cleared by anglers, guides us to the river. It only takes a year, without visitors, for the clearing to disappear.

The flow of water, through Coto Puente de Ortega, is regulated by a reservoir, called Embalse de Tranco, and this circumstance creates different types of swims, in our part of the fishing reserve, depending mainly on the amount of water discharged from the dam. A long trip often ends in disappointment when the water level is found to be high, but in our case the same unpromising conditions resulted in a good days' fishing.

Most of the time high water levels make many months of the season impossible to fish. High water levels coincide with demand for water for irrigation. If you're not familiar with the local pattern then the best thing is to fish with a friend who does or simply wait for a better moment; and in any case prudence comes before any trout. If in doubt compare water levels, shown in the photos, with your own experiences.

Satisfying captures help the day to pass, with a fantastic feeling

As the morning proceeds it gets hotter despite being the middle of October, and I place my hope in small clouds appearing overhead that lower the humidity. It's a great experience to feel part of nature standing in a beautiful river; and most of our body is water.

The photos, shown here, can only hint at the beauty of the Guadalquiver valley and Sierra Cazorla. You have to make the journey yourself to fully realize what a special experience fly fishing in Jaén really can be.

To wish the fishing season goodbye causes a little heartache, but let's make the best of what remains. I feel butterflies in my stomach, as I place my fly lure near to a submerged boulder, imagining a fish to leave from the deep, against the current, strong, and vigorous and fearlessly attacking my fly lure.

Watch out! Water is released from a dam and the river level rises quickly

But it didn't happen this way, instead the line planed, slowly and smoothly, falling to the edge of some foam. I spotted, from the first moment, a doubtful shadow rising, swimming below, positioning to take the fly and my thoughts, forming in my mouth, almost like an athlete "we go, we go". Nothing is certain, and the fly lure can sometimes catch a rock instead, but his time the trout attacked, I waded into the water to celebrate my first fish. The best catch of the day, and to say goodbye until next year.

Straight after releasing the fish several good size trout began to jump near me, they ignored my fly lure cast in front of them. They imitate a fireworks castle and I'm left a spectator to their fun. Perhaps they're celebrating the end of the fishing season too?

As you can see, from the pictures, Coto Puente Ortega has many faces and the majority of them depend on the volume of water in the river. But above all else she is like no other place, distinguished by gorges that water has cut through the valley.

A fishing pool is found on the upstream part of Puente Ortega fishing reserve

My catches were of average size. Not very big but I have to admit that these fish never leave me bored – for one second, something practically impossible, in a river with a tremendous variety of swims found throughout the fishing reserve.

There's no need to hurry, fish slowly and methodically. It's very important to relax, leave anxiety in the car and count up to ten before beginning. If we follow this rule then the river can reward us but if you don't, elusive trout will punish our mistakes. In spite of everything it is difficult not to watch the river and expect a catch from the next bend in the channel.

The temperature was ideal, not too hot although, towards the end of the afternoon, short sleeves offered little protection. Isolated gusts of wind infrequently obstructed my view, but then quickly disappeared.

Gaudalquiver valley, Jaén   A great symbol for Spain

Trout take advantage of any position in which the current has lots of oxygen and brings them easy food. I attempt to place the fly lure, unnoticed, in front of the boulder, where a trout holds up but in spite of my best efforts the fish had disappeared.

It's difficult to conceal yourself, in the pool shown in the previous photo. You can spot the fish and they can see you at the same time. The sun is a wonderful companion that allows us to see our fly lure with clarity, since we need to cast it a relatively long way if we don't want to become a hostage to the crystal clear water."

▶ Coto Puente Ortega has more than one face

Compare the left hand image, of a rock found in our valley, with surrealist artist Jeff Koon's great art work created, by the roundabout, outside the Guggenheim Museum in Bilbao.

River Madera

21. **Coto Don Marcos**, day ticket required, low mountain-water fishing rules apply, Siles, Benatae and Torres de Albanchez (rainbow trout) ten anglers are permitted to fish each day along a 9.9km stretch from a road-bridge connecting Segura with Siles downstream until a road bridge connecting Torres de Albanchez with Benatae. Day tickets are available from the park's office, Oficina Del Parque de Cazorla Tel, 953 72 01 02.

22. **Coto Madera Bajo**, day ticket required, river Madera - downstream stretch, brown trout, Santiago-Pontones and Segura de la Sierra (brown trout) six anglers are permitted to fish each day along a 5.6km stretch from the forestry commission lake office called Casa Forestal de la Laguna downstream until the confluence with the river Segura. Fly fishing only with a single barbless hook is allowed. Day tickets are available from the town hall - Ayuntamiento de Santiago Pontones Tel, 953 43 80 02 and the Oficina Del Parque de Cazorla Tel, 953 72 01 02.

Embalse de la Anchuricas is a trout fishing water, a day ticket is required. The reservoir has an idyllic setting among wooded shoreline. It's located in the municipality of Santiago-Pontones and fishing is permitted from the third Sunday in March until 30th November. Artificial fly lures, ground bait and sweetcorn are allowed. Provincial bag limit applies for trout. A popular spot is by the dam wall where trout are often are hooked using teaspoon spinning lures. Barbel and carp are caught here as well.

20. **Coto Huelga del Nidillo**, river Borosa, day ticket required, low mountain-water fishing rules apply, catch and release, Santiago-Pontones and La Iruela (brown trout) six anglers are permitted to fish each day along a 3.5km stretch from the power station-bridge called 'puente de la Central del Salto de los Organos' downstream until Charco Pancica Bridge. Only fly fishing is permitted, using a single barbless hook. Day tickets are available from the park's office, Oficina Del Parque de Cazorla Tel, 953 72 01 02. Trout are difficult to deceive at this pretty location.

23. **Coto El Duende** (Mogón), day ticket required, intensive fishing reserve rules apply, Villacarillo (rainbow trout). Fishing is permitted all year from Mogón aqueduct downstream until the second elevator station. Day tickets are available from the park's office, Oficina Del Parque de Cazorla Tel, 953 72 01 02.

24. **Coto de Sillero**, day ticket required, low mountain-water fishing rules apply, catch and release, Villacarillo (brown trout) six anglers are permitted to fish each day from the third Sunday in March until 12th October along a 10.4km stretch from puente de la Gorda downstream until Mogón aqueduct. Day tickets are available from the park's office, Oficina Del Parque de Cazorla Tel, 953 72 01 02.

Free fishing for trout in mountain streams, classed as 'agues libres trucheras de alta montaña', takes place at the following locations.

- **River Guadalquiver**: fish from Herrerias Bridge towards Vadillo Castril Bridge, flyfishing only with a single barbless hook.

- **River Aguascebas Grande**: fish from the confluence with Aguascebas Chico stream towards the confluence with Aguascebas de la Cueva stream, fly fishing only with a single barbless hook.

- **River Madera** (Segura River basin): fish from Peca stream until the forestry office, called casa forestal da La Laguna, fly fishing only with a single barbless hook.

- **River Zumeta**: fish from Fuenesca Bridge towards a dam, sign-posted 'Presa de Palomares'.

No fishing areas are sign-posted 'refugios de pesca' or 'acotoda de pesca'.

Upstream boundary of the River Poqueira at Poqueira hydroelectric power-station, go to page 93 for a description of this free fishing, catch and release, high mountain trout reserve

Vocabulary

Eight further titles, in Phil's Fishing Guide Books series, are available in

e-Book format, and paperback from the author's webpage:
www.spainfishing.com

- **The Essential Guide to Coarse Fishing in Spain**. ISBN: 8489954496
  Reviewed by the Angling Times, they said "This book contains excellent
  information on all the Costa areas and Canary Islands. Plus the
  Guadiana and Tajo rivers in Extremadura: and northern
  Spain's river Duero. This book deals with top fishery locations, obtaining
  a fishing licence, and also offers best fishing methods.

- **The Smooth Guide to Coarse Fishing in Southern France**.
  ISBN: 9780954692489 covers the Saone, Rhone, Lot, Tarn and
  Dordogne rivers and the regions of Gironde, Haute-Vienne in Limoges,
  Aveyron, the Pyrenees and Provence plus much more.

- **The Smooth Guide to Coarse Fishing in Northern France**.
  ISBN: 095469242X. Reviewed by the Angler's Mail in August 2004, they
  said, "The guidebook concentrates on the exact information you want
  from this type of guide and covers those rivers and lakes that can be
  fished simply by buying a fishing licence".

- **The Smooth Guide to Fly Fishing in France**. ISBN: 9780954692470,
  covers fishing for sea trout in Normandy, Atlantic salmon in Brittany,
  Arctic char, brook trout, Lake and rainbow trout from mountain lakes in
  the Pyrenees and brown trout in Central France.

- **The Smooth Guide to Fishing in Portugal**. ISBN: 9780954692414 it
  covers coarse, game and sea fishing. The Angler's Mail said in their ****
  star review "The book highlights favourite places to coarse, game and
  sea fish all over Portugal from the Algarve located in the south to
  the river Douro located in the north. Expert advice is given about
  licences, tackle and tactics".

Northern Spain's world famous fly fishing rivers and lakes are explored in the following four titles.

- **The Smooth Guide to Fly Fishing in Asturias (Northern Spain).**
  ISBN: 13: 9780954692452. Spain's Atlantic salmon fishing hotspot. Also good for brown, rainbow and sea trout.

- **The Smooth Guide to Fly Fishing in Galicia (North West Spain).**
  ISBN: 13: 9780954692445. Spain's' premier sea trout fishing destination. Also good for brown trout and American largemouth Black bass fishing.

- **The Smooth Guide to Fly Fishing in Castile and León Northern-Central Spain (León, Salamanca and Zamora).**
  ISBN: 13: 9780954692469. Includes fishing for Huchen (freshwater salmon) but also brown trout, pike and barbel.

- **The Smooth Guide to Fly Fishing in North East Spain (La Rioja, Navarra, Aragón and Catalonia).** Fishing for wild brown trout and barbel in the Pyrenees. ISBN: 9780957281202.

Each paperback is approximately 150 pages, A5 size, and perfect bound, in paperback. Cost is around twelve pounds plus postage.

For further information or copies:
E-mail address: philippembroke007@hotmail.com

The author's Web page: www.spainfishing.com contains excellent information about all his fishing guide book titles, free to download Spanish fishing sketch maps and expert information on fishing holidays abroad.

Scientific References

• Journal of Fish Diseases Volume 14 Issue 5, Page 545 - September 1991

• Journal of Fish Diseases Volume 23 Issue 4, Page 295 - July 2000

• Journal of Fish Diseases Volume 29 Issue 6, Page 339 - June 2006

• Fisheries Management and Ecology Volume 11 Issue 3-4, Page 145 - June 2004

• Journal of Freshwater Biology Volume 41 Issue 4, Page 707 - June 1999

• Journal of Freshwater Biology, Volume 51 Issue 6, Page 1175 - June 2006

• Ecology of Freshwater Fish volume 8, issue 3, page 151, September 1999

Vocabulary

▼A-Z of Fly Fishing in Spain

►USEFUL WORDS

Agua alta montaña: upstream water
Alevinage: fish fry
Anzuelo: hook
Arponcillo: barb
Arriba/superior: upstream
Arroyo: stream
Au toc: traditional bait fishing
Autoctona: wild brown trout
Azud: lock or dam
Bajo/inferior: downstream
Balsa: irrrigation pond
Banzao/Vanzao/Trabenco: water behind wall/weir
Bastane: barley
Bechoco: larvae
Besbello; damsel/dragonfly nymph
Buldó: plastic bubble float
Boya lastrada: ballasted bubble float
Cabeza: metallic ballast used to form head of nymph or streamer fly lure
Cacho: Pyrenean dace
Caña de pescar: fishing rod
Caenis: caddis
Captura y suelta – catch and release
Cebada: barley
Cebo: bait
Charco: pond
Chipa: small, fish species
Chuteto: fish slide
Cuenca: river basin
Culo de pato: cul de canard
Curricán: trolling
Cierre: lock

Cola de rata: fly line leader
Coto de pesca: fishing reserve
Coto sin muerte: catch and release zone
Coto tradicional: trout zone
Corriente: riffle
Desague; overflow drain
Descanso: landing platform
Desembocadura: exit into large water
Depuradora: water purifier plant
Escalada: waterfull
Escalo: European chub
Escuala de pesca: fishing school
Esguin: smolt
Estrecho: river stretch
Frezadero: spawning ground
Furtivismo: poaching
Gravera: canalised channel
Gusano: worm
Hucho: Huchen salmon
Huesal: small Asturias river
Hueva: fish eggs
Lampreas: lamprey marine fish
Lance: shallow run
Latigo: casting
Lombriz: worm
Margen: bank
Meruco: lombriz (worm)
Molino: mill
Mosca: fly
Mosca ahogada: wet fly
Mosca seca: dry fly
Mosca de mayo: mayfly
Mújoles: mullet (Galician)
Nudo: knot
Orilla: bank

Pantano: small reservoir
Paracaídas: parachute fly
Para ribereños: only local anglers allowed to fish
Parados: eddy
Pasarela peatonal: footbridge
Pesca sin muerte: catch and release
Pesca a seca: dry fly fishing
Pesca libre: free fishing
Pesca mosca: flyfishing
Peso: weight
Pinto: parr
Piscifactoría: hatchery
Ploma: ledger weight
Pluma: feather
Pilastre: pillar
Posturas: fishing platform
Pozo: pool
Presa: dam
Presa muro: dam wall
Puente: bridge
Quisquilla: common prawn
Raseras: glide
Repobladas: stocked trout

Reo: sea trout
Regato: brook
Riada: flood
Ribereños: local anglers
Sábalo: shad
Saltamontes: grasshopper
Salto: weir
Sarnosa: wet fly lure made from a Gallo de León (cockerel feather)
Salvelino: brook trout
Seca: dry fly
Tablada/tabla: a water mass found behind a weir or other obstacle
Temporada de pesca: fishing season
Tirando: playing the fish
Tramo: river section
Tramo libre sin muerte: catch and release, free fishing stretch
Trucha aco-iris: rainbow trout
Trucha común: brown trout
Trucha marisca: sea trout
Vado; ford
Vedado: no-fishing area

Technical assistance gratefully accepted from: James Hunter (Inverness Fisheries Department) who enjoys fishing in Spain.

Conversion Chart

When weighing your catches, remember:
1 kilogram (kg) equals 2.2 pounds (lb)
5 kilogram's equal 11 pounds
1 pound equals 453 grams
5 pounds equal 2.5 kilogram's